THE PROGRAMMER'S
ALGOL

THE PROGRAMMER'S ALGOL: A Complete Reference

CHARLES PHILIP LECHT

President, Advanced Computer Techniques Corporation

With a foreword by
ROBERT BEMER, *General Electric Company*

New York
San Francisco
Toronto
London   M c G R A W - H I L L   B O O K   C O M P A N Y
Sydney

*For Meg and her dolls so they can speak
in a language the Guinea pigs can't understand*

FOREWORD

Among my ALGOL memorabilia are two comic strips from the London Daily
Express. On June 28, 1961 the hero of future space adventures, Jeff
Hawke, says,

> "According to my capsule, a space-horse is a pilgrim ship, and
> can do no wrong! It carries pilgrims to the ancient oracle in
> the system of Algol. The voyage takes fifty years. Once on
> board, one never gets off..."

On June 30 we find a rather shady character exclaiming,

> "But-the-journey-to-Algol-takes-fifty-years!"

To which his female companion replies,

> "So what? At least you'll live to see the end of it..."

So much buried philosophy applicable to programming has not been seen
since Alice in Wonderland. In particular it reminds us that for so
long a voyage one should keep a log, if only for one's children.

The advent of this reference book on ALGOL has suggested to me that
I should compile such a log, or chronicle of events and the forces
that shaped them. Progress reports on ALGOL have been published in
the professional and commercial journals of information processing,
but they have been fragmentary for the most part and limited to what
could be made public in a time of many heated controversies. Today
the lava has cooled somewhat and a fuller and perhaps more dispassion-
ate account is in order.

Thus, at the present time I am compiling an ALGOL history. This
FOREWORD represents a careful selection and abridgement of items contained within my vast file of notes. I hope, then, that the reader
will understand that the following material represents but a short
history of ALGOL's "long journey."

ALGOL was started with high hopes for both universalism and efficacy.
The first occurred slowly because of business practicality, the slowness
of communication in such a large field, and the lack of a controlling
body. The second lagged because such a language matures slowly, being
dependent upon actual experience and usage for feedback and improvement.
Some of the U. S. participants in defining ALGOL 60 had just returned
from Paris when a so-called "rump" group demonstrated just what ambigu-
ities they had approved without realizing it.

One can give several reasons for this slow maturation. They are:
1] Ineffective description - The advantages and power of ALGOL (perhaps
as compared to FORTRAN) were not obvious to all because the desirable
nature of its improved logical rigor and generality were not publicized

effectively. The first, and perhaps the fortieth, description of
the language was couched in such terms as to repel the practicing
programmer, particularly in the U. S. That this trepidation was due to
the form of presentation was illustrated strikingly by Rabinowitz'
paper "Report on the Algorithmic Language FORTRAN II," in the 62 June
issue of the Communications of the ACM. The title is identical to that
of the Paris report except for the name of the language, and the description is given correspondingly in Backus Normal Form. As such, it looks
far more forbidding than ALGOL; at the very least it demonstrates many
more exceptions and structural faults.

Supporters of the language were in agreement that action was needed
and some arguments were made that usage was not really that difficult.
More than this, correct ALGOL usage seemed easier to achieve. Other
attempts were made to popularize the presentation, but the flexi-
bility and power obviously frightened the average practitioner.

2] Difference in orientation between the U. S. and Europe - In 1958 the
volume of work done with a formula language in Europe was only a frac-
tion of that in the U. S., roughly paralleling the disparity in numbers
of computers in use. Thus, a reasonably fresh start was possible. The
U. S. community felt much more practical and suspected the Europeans
of idealism. Indeed, some naivete was apparent in assuming that whole-
sale adoption of ALGOL in Europe implied full international acceptance.
By numbers of countries, yes; by number of users, no. Five years
later there will not be an ISO standard for the language, for requirements for such a standard transcend what was envisioned in 1958, or
even 1961.

ALGOL should have progressed more rapidly, for the powerful SHARE organization certainly gave it initial support. They had plans to stop
further modifications to FORTRAN and adopt ALGOL. Yet later they with-
drew acceptance and proceeded with FORTRAN IV, even though that language
was also incompatible with its predecessor. Primarily this was due to
a vested interest in FORTRAN programs. FORTRAN had the head start and
simply grew in volume at the faster rate.

Whereas the U. S. Government gave strong support to the COBOL language,
for business work, they did not for ALGOL. In contrast, the German
Research Council desired that all computers at German universities be
equipped with ALGOL processors as a condition of ordering. Since it
reportedly provides 95% of the monetary support for this purpose, the
support is assumed to be strong.

3] Accent on production - ALGOL came on the scene when the U. S. users
were engaged in a struggle to achieve production to justify all the
expensive computer equipment they had ordered for advertising purposes
and keeping up with the Joneses. Thus, most ALGOL processors were
experimental at a time when FORTRAN was well into production. This
pushed FORTRAN from version I into II, where subroutines already con-
verted into machine language were able to be called for execution by
a FORTRAN program. In many cases these pre-compiled subroutines may

have been written in another procedure language, such as COBOL. Some
installations even made a practice of using FORTRAN as a linkage
skeleton, with the main part of the working program written in other
languages. Such usage was not applied in volume to ALGOL, and some
claimed that it could not be done.

4] Ineffective maintenance – ALGOL was the first language attempted
originally on an international scale. FORTRAN was mostly under the
control of a single manufacturer and COBOL was under firm industry
supervision. ALGOL, however, was opened to all who had an interest.
This led to heterogeneous membership in maintenance groups, many of
who's members had no conception of what the term "maintenance" meant
to the others. This led to the abortive Oak Ridge proposal. Universities and research centers did not have the same requirements as
a manufacturer, who can pay heavy contractual penalties if software
does not perform properly. In this case it becomes "properly according to whom?"

This was the problem facing IBM, who's recognized leadership in the
computer field might have put ALGOL over sooner had they been so
inclined. IBM ALGOL was available, consisting of ALGOL where ALGOL
and FORTRAN did the same function, and FORTRAN where ALGOL was lacking,
such as in input-output statements. But formal control was lacking.
Also, IBM seemed to wisely avoid the political situation and while
they could have, they did not wish to usurp control. Better to be
prudent than risk the vagaries of someone "actively engaged in writing
programs in the ALGOL 60 language" and who has a committee vote equivalent to that of IBM!

This was finally expressed with sufficient strength and control was
vested in IFIPS, a responsible body which has mounted an excellent
effort leading to resurgence in ALGOL.

5] Restrictions on character set available – The expanded character
set of ALGOL (over 100 at a graphic per symbol, such as ? for if)
appeared far in advance of hardware which could handle it properly.
The obvious device of a publication and reference language did not
suffice in actuality. The ALCOR group felt this problem strongly.
Predictions were ignored and then the users found out. Meanwhile the
development of the ISO (ASCII) code was taking place. Double case
alphabets are still rare, though Teletype may announce such a terminal
in 1966. A proposal was made to reserve a set of control characters
following the ESCape character for programming language usage, but
this was never understood or followed up.

6] Lack of input-output provisions – This has been a very real deter-
rent to the acceptance of ALGOL for production computation. Fortunately
some excellent work appeared at a critical time which has significantly
alleviated the problem.

Then what has been the benefit of ALGOL, if any? Many things:

1] Interest - It provided the first big vehicle for international dis-
cussions on a commonly developed computer language in the computing
field and put a lot of people to thinking. It was acclaimed, damned
and then treated respectfully with the growth of fuller understanding.
Until the end of 1960, Datamation (persumably the leading U. S. peri-
odical in the field) took very little public notice. Around the end
of 1961 the interest started to run high and was maintained through
1964, gradually decreasing from that point.

2] A decided effect upon computer design - The English Electric KDF9
and the Burroughs B5000 series came on the market at roughly the same
time, both using devices sometimes labelled as "pushdown" stores.
Both groups of designers were surprised to find the other's usage, and
it can be attributed directly as an ALGOL spinoff. Dijkstra is often
credited for the "stack" from his 60 October paper in Numerische
Mathematik, but the earliest manifestation is due to Bauer and
Samelson. These two, giants in the ALGOL field among many others,
must be credited for originating the "cellar" principle in their 1959
paper on Sequential Formula Translation, in English in the Communications
of the ACM, 60 February. A salute to these two good friends.

3] Understandable algorithms for human and machine interchange - The
interest of most numerical analysts has been captured by the possibility
of describing their processes in a way that is at the same time very
readable for understanding and suitable for machine translation on a
variety of equipment to produce working programs which perform the
process. A relatively large number of algorithms have been published
in:

      Communications of the ACM (USA)   B. I. T. (Scandinavia)

      The Computer Journal/Bulletin (UK)   ALGORYTMY (USSR)

      Numerische Mathematik (Germany)

Also in Selected Numerical methods (Gram), and

      Computer Programs for Physical Chemistry (Maine and Seawright)

Indexes of algorithms have been published in the Communications of
the ACM, in the issues for 62 January, 64 March, 64 December and 65
December. Apparently missing is the "Taschenbuch," to be a handbook
in five or more volumes published by Springer-Verlag. Designed to be
a compendium of numerical knowledge capsulated in the ALGOL language
mentioned publicly at least as early as 59 December, this has not been
available in the U. S., at least. Possibly a sufficient body of
algorithms has not yet been accumulated in a comprehensive manner.

x

4] As a construction language and for superstructures - I stated in 1962, at the Armour Research Symposium, that "languages of the future, whether or not they be outgrowths, modifications or adaptations of our present languages, will survive only on the basis of being both intro- spective and reproductive. They must have the facility to talk about themselves and specify their processor in their own language." ALGOL has been more successful than most in this area. van der Poel offered at the Rome meeting to supply a version of ALGOL written essentially in ALGOL. Burroughs did their B5000 ALGOL in this manner, and so did Bull G. E. for the 600; more than this, it has been used as a con- struction language for other processors.

Both FORTRAN and ALGOL have been used as bases for superstructures of other programs, both applications and other languages. An exceptional example of this is SIMULA, done by the Norwegian Computing Centre, which is both connective to and written in ALGOL. It is my opinion that ALGOL has so far lent itself more suitably for this purpose than any competitor of standing.

5] As a language for new generations of computers - We speak here of ALGOL X and Y, being developed as successors to ALGOL 60. There was formerly an inexpressible and intuitive feeling by ALGOL proponents that the elegant and simple structure was of great value but this just could not be shown to enough advantage to convince FORTRAN users. Multiprocessing, multiprogramming, reactive operation, time-sharing and real-time environments provided the crucial evaluation. The basic power of ALGOL is more evident now that facilities must be provided in a language to handle this new complication. This was evident in IBM's switch to a new language with many of the features of ALGOL. However, IFIP has not been relaxing in its role of custodian for ALGOL. The language ALGOL X shows many differences from ALGOL 60. For example, Naur has proposed an environment and data division. The lesson of 1959 COMTRAN has been learned.

6] Dispelling a myth - At the beginning of the ALGOL effort, SHARE was promoting UNCOL, or UNiversal Computer Oriented Language. The men from UNCOL do not seem much in evidence these days. The first APIC Annual Review in Automatic Programming has an article indicating that no UNCOL processors were running, due to the fact that language spec- ifications were incomplete. One wonders where it is after these eight years; apparently the last published paper was that in the 62 January Computer Bulletin.

One hesitates to compare it to the philosopher's stone, however, because up just one level we have successful processors being contructed by special purpose language-development languages (POPS).

A few quantitative measurements are perhaps useful to round out this history:

1] Interest in ALGOL has been international from its inception.
Recently, however, the circle of interested countries has expanded.
The mailing list in issue #19 of the ALGOL Bulletin included recip-
ients in:

Australia	Czechoslovakia	Italy	Sweden
Austria	Denmark	Japan	Switzerland
Belgium	France	Netherlands	U. K.
Canada	Germany W.	Norway	U. S. A.
China	Germany E.	Poland	U. S. S. R.

This very "one world" group was augmented in the very next issue by:

Brazil, Finland, the Irish Republic, Israel and Rumania.

This same ALGOL Bulletin is the best way to note the progress of ALGOL X
and Y.

Only the serious should apply, but copies may be obtained by writing
either:

The Mathematical Centre, 2e Boerhaavestraat 49, Amsterdam - 0,
the Netherlands (attention Mr. M. F. Calisch), or

Mr. P. Z. Ingerman, RCA, EDP Bldg. 204-2, Camden, New Jersey 08101, USA

2] ALGOL is sometimes considered to have fathered a number of variants
such as MAD, JOVIAL, CPL, NELIAC, BALGOL, ALPHA, etc., whereas FORTRAN
is often presumed to be pristine. About the only difference I can see
is that the authors of the ALGOL variants gave them different names,
while the authors of the FORTRAN variants for the most part retained
the name. One survey of the different FORTRANs (prior to ASA stand-
ardization) showed over a dozen, of which eight existed within IBM.
Then too, FORTRAN II is quite different from FORTRAN I, and FORTRAN IV
goes so far as to be actually incompatible with FORTRAN II.

3] In comparing ALGOL to FORTRAN we note the following:
    a] From a publication and paper viewpoint, the KWIC index to the
AFIPS Conferences, 1951-1964, show two papers on ALGOL and one on
FORTRAN (the original), and is inconclusive. The KWIC index to
Computing Reviews (ACM), 1960-1963, shows 49 papers on ALGOL to 11
on FORTRAN, but this is certainly equalized by the fact that FORTRAN
is by far the earlier language. It arrived at a time when most of
the present journals in information processing, such as the Communications of the ACM, were non-existent, and naturally most of the papers
would arise during the earliest life of a programming language.
    b] From the standpoint of the number of published algorithms,
ALGOL holds a commanding lead.

c] The number of books and texts could be considered roughly equal.

d] When last surveyed, the number of processors for various computers was about equal (CACM, 63 March). Despite a formal request through the ALGOL Bulletin, the ISO survey has not been updated in this area. W. McClelland, Director of the ISO/TC97/SC5 survey at the time of its publication, reports that lack of information forced the disbandment of that subgroup. However, the number of ALGOL processors has certainly increased considerably since that time, possibly more in proportion than FORTRAN. The 64 July ALGOL Bulletin reports 8 compilers in use in Japan, with 4 more under construction, where the original survey showed none.

e] The comparative numbers of users can only be estimated, based upon such information which showed FORTRAN programs at about ten times the number of ALGOL programs (for the U. S. only), but we would guess perhaps that only four times as many FORTRAN programmers exist, which seems quite remarkable in view of the previous quantitative comparisons.

Concluding, I commend ALGOL and its future to the independent thinkers like Professor Galler. If something proves practical and of substance, use it, but not for the sake of nationalism, entrenchment or prejudice. ALGOL, in its many manifestations and effects, has won a secure place in information processing history.

R. W. BEMER

PREFACE

And so another has undertaken the task of preparing an ALGOL book. As might be expected, the idea to do so was born in a desire to "do it better." The task of accumulating the material, formatting it, etc. was formidable.

This book is different from others in that its presentation of ALGOL has been carefully chosen to provide the programmer with a description of the language, graduated from the simplest to the most complex forms of its elements. Thus, the ten statements and declarations of ALGOL have been expanded to appear as though they, hence ALGOL itself, were composed of many more "instructions." The purpose in doing this was to reduce the usual high level of inference and deduction required of programmers utilizing the highly general forms traditionally encountered in ALGOL presentations.

It must be pointed out to those who read this book that the main intent in its development was for use as a reference source. This does not preclude its use in the classroom. Indeed, the converse is true. Since the fundamental rules of usage of most compiler languages can be presented very quickly, classroom instruction involves, for the most part, the extensive coding of contrived problems. In this way, the beginner "learns" the language.

The practicing programmer, the audience to whom this book is directed, is frustrated by the presentation of computer languages in books, manuals, etc. intended to serve the multi-purpose task of being an introductory exposé, a classroom text, a reference source, and a what-have-you, simultaneously. Thus, ALGOL programmers or programmers learning ALGOL will find this book most valuable when faced with the task of actually programming.

This book has been derived from a manual prepared by Advanced Computer Techniques Corporation (ACT), New York, New York, for the General Electric Company entitled "GE-625/635 ALGOL," March 1966. Maximum recognition must be given to Mrs. Winnie Schare whose tireless efforts accumulated a major portion of the book's material. In addition, Miss Joan Gildea managed a singularly professional technical typing effort receiving substantial help from Miss Katherine Majewski and others.

New York
Charles Philip Lecht

Guide to the Effective Use of This Book

This book contains a carefully planned description of the ALGOL language. The words "carefully planned" are used to emphasize the unique structure and presentation format of the subject material. It is intended that this structure and format be thoroughly understood by the reader before using the book for its major purpose--as a reference source--or for any additional purposes (e.g., as a course text). This section provides the information necessary for such an understanding.

At the onset, it is important to note that a distinction must be made between the <u>definition and structure of ALGOL</u> and the <u>facilities</u> which ALGOL allows its implementors in innovation of highly individualized additions to its instruction repertoire. Thus, the six ALGOL STATEMENTS and four ALGOL DECLARATIONS presented are to be viewed as members of the instruction repertoire set in <u>all</u> ALGOL compilers. Such items as input/output procedures, mathematical functions, etc.* are the personalized innovations of compiler implementators. These find their development motivations in the specific hardware and/or software environments within which a particular ALGOL compiler is intended to be used.

The various national and international committees responsible for preparing a definition of ALGOL which will be accepted by the international computer community have been the guardians of "a measure" by which ALGOL implementors and users can gauge the faithfulness of "their version" (as well as delineate inter-compiler differences). It must be pointed out that frequently there are wide differences between committee idealisms and pragmatic realities, the main causes of which may be found in commercial motivations. But, this is not a new concept. It is written here to remind the ALGOL theorist that, as it is with all widely used computer languages, the concept of ALGOL as a working compiler possesses two major qualifications: what it is to a specific implementation group and what it is to the International Standards Organization.

The definition of the ALGOL language as presented in this book has been derived through study of <u>existing</u> compilers. In light of this fact, the reader must be made aware that while Sections III STATEMENTS and IV DECLARATIONS may be seen to be almost universally implemented and understood as being standard in <u>all</u> ALGOL compilers, the remaining text may and often does contain ideas not to be found with such frequency. Indeed,

---

*   It has been rumored that ALGOL implementors do not always agree on these items not to speak of the content, form, manipulative characteristics, and means of writing the statements and declarations themselves.

the inclusion of such material is intended to convey to users of this
book that while the STATEMENTS and DECLARATIONS are in themselves very
powerful computational and data processing tools, writing a computer
program in ALGOL implies the usage of <u>other</u> language members.

Thus, if these "additional" language members are not identical to those
found in some specific ALGOL compilers the reason for their inclusion
is clear. Also, they should help the reader understand analogous concepts which he may encounter.

This book is a reference manual for programmers. It is not intended to
be a primer or introductory exposition on how to write computer programs
in general or on the ALGOL language in particular. It may be used to
learn the language; however, this presupposes that the reader is familiar
with the basic machine and language independent principles of computer
programming.

To use this book for educational purposes the reader must be aware of
the implications of the above paragraphs, i.e., the particular compiler
which he may want to use may not function in exactly the same way as the
description of the one which is contained in this book.

ALGOL is characterized by having relatively few distinct instructions*
(statements and declarations) in comparison with other compiler languages
(e.g., FORTRAN). The power of the language derives from its great flexi-
bility in allowing many variations of each instruction form.

Traditionally, ALGOL books and manuals have dwelled upon the generalized
forms of each instruction in the language repertoire after having presented
definitions of terms, concepts, etc. The various derivable forms of the
instructions which the user needs to implement an application were learned
<u>by inference</u> in the remaining text and through examples. Much was
learned "on the computer."

This book overcomes the problem of providing insight into the variations
possible with each instruction. Thus, each is presented as a series of
variations proceeding from the simplest to the most complex forms. This
provides the user with a wider insight into ALGOL's utilization possibil-
ities.

Each form is presented as though it were a separate and distinct member
of the ALGOL language. Each set of such forms is preceded by a title
page containing its generally accepted generic name. Finally, each form
starts on a new page and is appropriately labelled on an upper corner.

---

*   The word instruction has been avoided in the remainder of this book.
     This has been done because it conflicts with the notions of statement
     and declaration as used in ALGOL.

It is important to note that these labels are not themselves generally accepted ALGOL names. They were developed to uniquely identify each of the forms given to each statement and declaration found in the standard ALGOL repertoire.

Chapter II serves as an index to locate each of the forms presented. This will aid the user in identifying a particular form as having been derived from one of the six statements or four declarations usually given, as well as direct him to a specific page in the text.

The general structure of this book is as follows:

Chapter I provides a definition and discussion of ALGOL. This includes a presentation of techniques and a detailed description of a sample ALGOL program.

Chapters II, III, IV and V describe the various ALGOL STATEMENTS and DECLARATIONS.

Chapter VI describes one commonly used version of INPUT/OUTPUT facilities available in ALGOL.

There are several Appendices in this book:

Appendix I discusses the concept of reserved identifiers.

Appendix II presents a list of mathematical functions available in most ALGOL compilers (by recommendation of the International Standards Organization).

Appendix III is a set of representative ALGOL programs derived from contributions to the Communications of the Association for Computing Machinery (ACM).

Appendix IV presents a glossary of terms. Each entry in this glossary has been chosen specifically because of its "need" vis-a-vis ALGOL. These definitions are for the most part derived from ALGOL '60 report.

There are several conventions which have been used in preparing this book. For example, the ALGOL language itself has been differentiated from its descriptive prose by the use of two type styles: manifold and italics, respectively. Each of the conventions is either clear by contextual use or is explained when necessary to understand the specific material affected by it.

CONTENTS

I. *Introduction*

A. DEFINITION AND STRUCTURE OF THE ALGOL LANGUAGE

Definition

ALGOL is an acronym for ALGOrithmic Language. The word "algorithm," as used here, implies ALGOL's unique capability as a tool for expressing problem solutions as efficient and precise procedures.

ALGOL is a language in which computer programs may be written.

ALGOL is a set of symbols and a set of rules. Associated with these are a set of definitions which are peculiar to a description of the language, its form and use.

There is a computer program associated with the ALGOL language. This program is called the "ALGOL compiler." All programs written in the ALGOL language must be processed by the ALGOL compiler prior to their execution as object programs.

Preparing a problem solution using the ALGOL language thus implies understanding the form and use of the language repertoire described in this book. In addition, an ALGOL compiler for translation of the source coding (i.e., the ALGOL program produced by the user of the language) into machine coding (i.e., the language of the computer itself) must be available.

This book does not discuss techniques in preparing an ALGOL compiler. This is stated to emphasise that its entire contents are dedicated to the presentation of procedures which must be followed by a programmer in preparing an ALGOL program for processing by an ALGOL compiler.

Structure

The structure of ALGOL is distinct from the structure of programs written in the ALGOL language. This section discusses the former while Section I B, *HOW TO WRITE AN ALGOL PROGRAM*, discusses the latter.

ALGOL is composed of statements and declarations.

Statements are used to specify operations to be performed by the computer in solving a problem.

Declarations provide the ALGOL compiler with information needed to define and link together various elements of the computer program during processing. In addition, the existence of declarations within the language facilitates the definition of program parameters.

The statements and declarations are composed of symbols. Note that some ALGOL symbols might conventionally be termed "character strings"; however, the definition of a symbol in ALGOL does not imply a single character. Also, certain symbols are enclosed in apostrophes. These apostrophes are a part of the symbol and must always appear when the symbol is used. *

Basic Symbols

a) letters - A B C D E F G H I J K L M N O P Q R S T U V W X Y Z
    letters are used for forming identifiers and strings.

b) digits - 0 1 2 3 4 5 6 7 8 9
    digits are used for forming numbers, identifiers and strings.

---

* The apostrophe is not used in this way in all ALGOL compilers. However, if it or some other type of delineator is not used to distinguish symbols which are used as part of the ALGOL language from those which may also be used within an ALGOL program as an identifier, such common usage could not occur.

c) *logical values* - 'TRUE' 'FALSE'

d) *arithmetic operators*

symbol	definition
+	addition
−	subtraction
*	multiplication
/	division
%	division
↑	exponentiation

e) *relational operators*

symbol	definition*
'LS'	less than (<)
'LQ'	less than or equal to ($\leq$)
'EQ'	equal to (=)
'GQ'	greater than or equal to ($\geq$)
'GR'	greater than (>)
'NQ'	not equal to ($\neq$)

f) *logical operators*

symbol	definition*
'EQV'	equivalent ($\equiv$)
'IMP'	implies ($\supset$)
'OR'	or ($\wedge$)
'AND'	and ($\vee$)
'NOT'	negation ($\neg$)

---

* The symbols shown in this column are frequently allowed for usage in place of those shown in the left hand column.

g) *punctuation* - *the following symbols have definite functions in the ALGOL language:*

symbol	definition	use
.	period	decimal point in numbers
,	comma	separator for items in a list
:	colon	separator for statement label
;	semicolon	separator for statements
(	left parenthesis	enclose parameter lists; indicate
)	right parenthesis	expression evaluation
[	left bracket	enclose subscripts
]	right bracket	
"	left string quote	enclose strings
\	right string quote	
'	apostrophe	indicate exponent
←	arrow	assignment operator
	blank space	space within strings

Note: Significant blanks are denoted by ƀ *in the text of this manual.*

h) *ALGOL words* - *the following words have a fixed meaning in the ALGOL language:*

'ARRAY'	'LABEL'
'BEGIN'	'OWN'
'BOOLEAN'	'PROCEDURE'
'COMMENT'	'REAL'
'DO'	'STEP'
'ELSE'	'STRING'
'END'	'SWITCH'
'FOR'	'THEN'
'GOTO'	'UNTIL'
'IF'	'VALUE'
'INTEGER'	'WHILE'

There are six types of statements available in ALGOL. Their names and a brief description of their functions follow:

<u>Statement Types</u>

<u>Name</u>	<u>Functions</u>
Assignment	To perform calculations and to assign a value to a variable or a group of variables
Conditional	To control the execution of individual statements or groups of statements
Dummy	To satisfy a programming protocol (described later) but it in itself performs no operation
'FOR'	To iterate a sequence of statements
'GOTO'	To transfer control
Procedure	To call a previously defined sequence of statements (e.g., a subroutine)

There are four types of declarations available in ALGOL. Their names and a brief description of their functions follow:

Declaration Types

Name	Functions
'ARRAY'	To define an array, specify its dimensions and its type
'PROCEDURE'	To define a subset of the computer program (e.g., a subroutine)
'SWITCH'	To specify control parameter which govern the sequence of program execution
Type	To specify the kind of value which a variable is to represent

There are many rules of protocol in writing an ALGOL statement or declaration. The major part of this manual discusses these.

The ALGOL language is structured in such a way as to impose rules of combining statements and segregating these as programs or subprograms in their own right. These concepts are presented in the section entitled, "COMPOUND STATEMENTS AND BLOCKS."

ALGOL does not contain statements which allow direct control of the input/output process. Thus, no statements or declarations exist for reading from or writing on external devices (e.g., READ, WRITE, etc., as in FORTRAN).

Since each implemented ALGOL compiler incorporates its own input/ output methods and these vary in their usage protocol (i.e., syntax, form, etc.), this book has elected to present the input/output implementation of one specific computer manufacturer's version. Thus, while the user of this book is reminded that its section on input/output (VI. INPUT/OUTPUT) is peculiar to one ALGOL compiler, study of it should allow for a better understanding of that which he may encounter elsewhere.

B. HOW TO WRITE AN ALGOL PROGRAM

The writing of any computer program presupposes an understanding of the problem to be solved and the selection of a programming language. Assuming these conditions to be satisfied, the following considerations are presented as a guide in the writing of ALGOL programs.

Form of an ALGOL Program

ALGOL programs are divided into logical sections called blocks. The entire program is also a block and must be enclosed within the symbols 'BEGIN' and 'END'. A block may contain any number of sub-blocks within it.

Variables, arrays, procedures and switches which are used in a block are defined in declarations at the beginning of the block. These declarations are followed by the statements of the block. Any statement of a block may in itself be a block (i.e., it must have block format as descrived in Section V) and thus blocks may be nested to any depth.

All ALGOL statements may be labelled with one or more statement labels, i.e., simple statements, compound statements and blocks may be labelled.

Execution of an ALGOL program starts with the first statement and continues successively from statement to statement. However, certain statements in the language have the power to change the sequence of statement execution.

Execution of the program is terminated when control reaches the 'END' symbol of the outermost block of the program.

The following diagram is given to suggest visually the structure of a typical (though arbitrary) ALGOL program. Each bracket denoted by ⌐'BEGIN' represents a block.
⌐'END'

The blocks are composed of declarations and statements (as discussed above). The declarations must precede the statements.

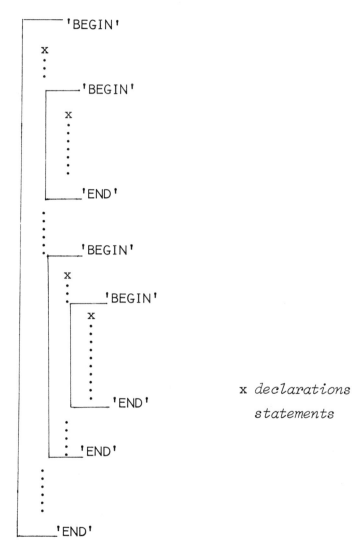

x declarations

statements

Note that this diagram represents an ALGOL program with three block levels and four blocks.

Writing Rules and Techniques

The ALGOL program may be written on coding forms designed specifically to handle the language.

Columns 1-72 of the coding form may be used for ALGOL statements and declarations.

The ALGOL code may appear anywhere within these columns.

The coding may appear in a completely free form. That is, any number of statements and/or declarations may appear on a single line.

A single statement or declaration may occupy as many lines as is desired.

Blanks may be used freely throughout the ALGOL code to improve the readability of the text. The only place in ALGOL in which blanks are significant is in strings. In all other instances they are disregarded by the compiler.

Since the line format of ALGOL programs is very flexible it is suggested that statement levels be indented on a new line to improve ease of reading and understanding a program.

Thus each new 'BEGIN' symbol may be indented at a new margin, and the 'END' corresponding to the 'BEGIN' may be placed at the same margin. Also, since statements may contain other statements, each lower statement level may be indented. When a higher level is resumed later on, statements for that level may be placed at the proper level margin (see form of the example given in Section I. C.).

It must be noted that these are merely suggestions which may be incorporated in order to make the program structure easy to follow. However, line indenting will in no way affect program execution.

Punctuation

When writing ALGOL statements and declarations there are two important rules of punctuation which must be employed.

Rule 1. The symbol ; is used between statements and between declarations. However, the semi-colon may be omitted after the last simple statement of a compound statement or block. The symbol 'END' serves as a statement separator in this case.

Examples

1. A←2; 'GOTO' Z

2. 'BEGIN' 'INTEGER' A; 'REAL' B;
    A←5.3; B←7.2 'END'

Rule 2. The symbol : is used to separate a statement label from a statement.

Examples

1. L: A←B+C; P: 'GOTO' R

2. T: 'BEGIN' I←I+1; J←J+1 'END'

Comments

If it is desired to place comments within the text of an ALGOL program, it may be done as follows:

To insert a comment between statements or declarations, or at the beginning of a compound statement or a block, the comment must be enclosed within the symbols 'COMMENT' and ;

Examples

1. A←B; 'COMMENT' COMPUTING C; C←A

2. 'BEGIN' 'COMMENT' COMPUTING C;
    A←B; C←A 'END'

To place a comment after a compound statement or a block (i.e., after the symbol 'END') the symbol 'COMMENT' is not necessary. A semi-colon must be used after the text if an 'END' or 'ELSE' symbol does not appear.

Examples

1. 'BEGIN' A←B; C←A 'END'
    COMPUTING D;
    D←C

2. 'IF' A 'LS' B 'THEN'
    'BEGIN' A←B; C←A 'END'
    COMPUTING C D IF A LS B
    'ELSE' B←A

Study of the examples provided with the detailed descriptions of the ALGOL statements and declarations in Chapters III and IV should aid in the understanding of how ALGOL statements are formed, punctuated, etc.

C. EXAMPLE OF AN ALGOL PROGRAM

This section contains a sample ALGOL Program.

The purpose of the program is to merge two sets of numbers. The two sets are contained in locations $a(1)$, $a(2)$,...,$a(i)$,..., $a(n)$ and $b(1)$, $b(2)$,...,$b(j)$,...,$b(m)$. The numbers in each set are assumed to be arranged in increasing order. The merged set is contained in locations $c(1)$, $c(2)$,..., $c(k)$,... .

The program operates as follows. The elements of arrays $\underline{a}$ and $\underline{b}$ are compared. At each comparison, the smaller element is put into the result array $\underline{c}$. When the end of either array $\underline{a}$ or $\underline{b}$ is reached, any remaining elements in the other array are put into the result array.

Symbols used in the program:

Symbol	Description
A	Identifier of input array
B	Identifier of input array
C	Identifier of output array
N	Subscript bound for array A
M	Subscript bound for array B
R	Subscript bound for array C
I	Subscript for array A
J	Subscript for array B
K	Subscript for array C
P	Controlled variable of 'FOR' statement

A listing of the program follows. The program is assumed to be a block contained in a larger block wherein the value of N, M and R are assigned, and wherein P is defined.

	Line
Program	

```
'BEGIN' 'ARRAY' A[1:N], B[1:M], C[1:R]; 'INTEGER' I, J, K;          100
I←J←K←1;                                                            110
START: 'IF' I 'GR' N 'THEN'                                         120
    'BEGIN' P←0; Q: C[K+P]←B[J+P]; P←P+1; 'IF' P 'LQ' M-J 'THEN''GO TO' Q 'END'   130
'ELSE' 'IF' J 'GR' M 'THEN'                                         140
    'BEGIN' P←0; S: C[K+P]←A[I+P]; P←P+1; 'IF' P 'LQ' N-I 'THEN' 'GO TO' S 'END'  150
'ELSE' 'BEGIN'                                                      160
    'IF' A[I] 'GQ' B[J] 'THEN'                                      170
        'BEGIN' C[K]←B[J]; J←J+1 'END'                              180
    'ELSE' 'BEGIN' C[K]←A[I]; I←I+1 'END';                          190
    K←K+1; 'GO TO' START                                            200
    'END'                                                           210
'END'                                                               220
```

A line by line description of this program appears on the following pages.

Line	Description
100	Contains 'BEGIN' for the block, and declarations of variables used.
110	Contains an assignment statement which sets I, J and K to the value 1.
120	Contains statement label "START" and the beginning of a conditional statement which extends to line 210. The 'IF' clause checks whether all of the elements of array A have been compared.
130	Contains the true branch of the 'IF' clause of line 120. The true branch is a compound statement which moves the remaining elements, if any, of array B to array C.
140	Contains the start of the false branch of the 'IF' clause of line 120. The false branch extends to line 210. The 'IF' clause in this line checks whether all of the elements of array B have been compared.
150	Contains the true branch of the 'IF' clause of line 140. The true branch is a compound statement which moves the remaining elements of array A to array C.
160	Contains the start of the false branch of the 'IF' clause of line 140. The false branch is a compound statement enclosed within 'BEGIN' and 'END' and extends to line 210.

Line	Description
170	Contains an 'IF' clause which compares elements of arrays A and B.
180	Contains the true branch of the 'IF' clause of line 170. The true branch is a compound statement which moves an element of array B to array C and then updates the B array subscript, J.
190	Contains the false branch of the 'IF' clause of line 170. The false branch is a compound statement which moves an element of array A to array C and then updates the A array subscript, I.
200	Contains an assignment statement to update the C array subscript, K, and a 'GOTO' statement to transfer control to the statement labelled "START."
210	Contains 'END' for the compound statement starting on line 160.
220	Contains 'END' for the block starting on line 100.

The structure of the conditional statement of the program is shown in Figure 1.

If the condition of line 120 is true, the true branch, line 130, is taken and subsequent control goes to line 210, i.e., the false branch is skipped. If the condition of line 120 is false, control goes to the false branch, line 140.

If the condition of line 140 is true, the true branch, line 150, is taken and subsequent control goes to line 210, i.e., the false branch is skipped. If the condition of line 140 is false, control goes to the false branch, line 160.

If the condition of line 170 is true, the true branch, line 180, is taken and subsequent control goes to line 210, i.e., the false branch is skipped. If the condition of line 170 is false, control goes to the false branch, line 190.

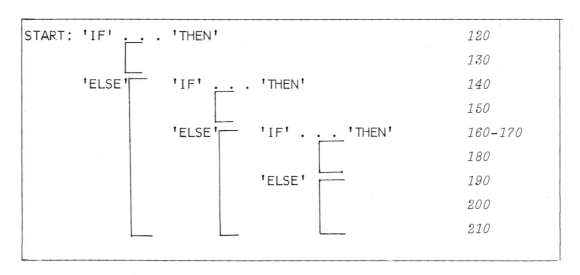

```
START: 'IF' . . . 'THEN'                                120
                                                        130
       'ELSE'    'IF' . . . 'THEN'                      140
                                                        150
                 'ELSE'    'IF' . . . 'THEN'            160-170
                                                        180
                           'ELSE'                       190
                                                        200
                                                        210
```

Figure 1. Outline of Conditional Statement

II. *Statement and Declaration Forms*

A. ASSIGNMENT STATEMENTS

B. CONDITIONAL STATEMENTS

B. CONDITIONAL STATEMENTS (cont'd)

Name	Form	Page
Conditional, n 'IF' clauses, 'ELSE'	'IF' b_1 'THEN' s_1 'ELSE' 'IF' b_2 'THEN' s_2 'ELSE' ... 'IF' b_{n-1} 'THEN' s_{n-1} 'ELSE' s_n	55

C. DUMMY STATEMENT

Name	Form	Page
Dummy	(null form)	59

D. 'FOR' STATEMENTS

Name	Form	Page
'FOR', expression	'FOR' $v \leftarrow e$ 'DO' s	63
'FOR', 'STEP' clause	'FOR' $v \leftarrow e_1$ 'STEP' e_2 'UNTIL' e_3 'DO' s	65
'FOR', 'WHILE' clause	'FOR' $v \leftarrow e$ 'WHILE' b 'DO' s	68
'FOR', general	'FOR' $v \leftarrow a_1, a_2, ..., a_n$ 'DO' s	70

E. 'GO TO' STATEMENTS

Name	Form	Page
'GO TO', label	'GO TO' a	75
'GO TO', switch designator	'GO TO' sw $[a]$	76
'GO TO', conditional designator	'GO TO' 'IF' b 'THEN' d_1 'ELSE' d_2	78

F. PROCEDURE STATEMENT

Name	Form	Page
Procedure statement	name $(a_1 \ t \ a_2 \ t \ \ldots \ t \ a_n)$	83

G. 'ARRAY' DECLARATIONS

Name	Form	Page
'ARRAY'	type 'ARRAY' $a_1, a_2, \ldots, a_n$	93
'ARRAY', 'OWN'	'OWN' type 'ARRAY' $a_1, a_2, \ldots, a_n$	96

H. 'PROCEDURE' DECLARATIONS

Name	Form	Page
'PROCEDURE' declaration, simple	'PROCEDURE' name $(a_1 \ t \ a_2 \ t \ \ldots \ t \ a_n)$; s	99
'PROCEDURE' declaration, specification part	'PROCEDURE' name $(a_1 \ t \ a_2 \ t \ \ldots \ t \ a_n)$; sp list; sp list;...; sp list; s	102
'PROCEDURE' declaration, value and specification part	'PROCEDURE' name $(a_1 \ t \ a_2 \ t \ \ldots \ t \ a_n)$; 'VALUE' list; sp list; sp list;...; sp list; s	105
'PROCEDURE' declaration, function definition	type 'PROCEDURE' name $(a_1 \ t \ a_2 \ t \ \ldots \ t \ a_n)$; 'VALUE' list; sp list; sp list;...; sp list; s	109

I.   'SWITCH' *DECLARATION*

Name	*Form*	*Page*
'SWITCH'	'SWITCH' $sw \leftarrow d_1, d_2, \ldots, d_n$	115

J.   *TYPE DECLARATIONS*

Name	*Form*	*Page*
Type	*type* $v_1, v_2, \ldots, v_n$	121
Type, 'OWN'	'OWN' *type* $v_1, v_2, \ldots, v_n$	123

The description of each statement and declaration in the ALGOL language
is presented in the following two sections. Each starts on a new page with
the format of its descriptive material given as shown below:

descriptive name

PURPOSE:

      (A brief statement of the purpose of the statement
      or declaration)

FORM:

      (Form of the statement or declaration)
                        (Definition of Symbols
                          used in the FORM line)

RULES:

      (A list of rules governing the correct usage of
      the statement or declaration; includes restrictions,
      suggestions, etc.)

EXAMPLES:

      (A list of examples illustrating the use of the
      statement or declaration)

III. *Statements*

Assignment Statements

PURPOSE:　To perform numerical calculations; to perform Boolean operations; to assign a value to one or more variables or procedure
identifiers in a single statement.

FORM:　　　　　$a_1 \leftarrow a_2 \leftarrow \ldots \leftarrow a_n \leftarrow e$

$a_1, a_2, \ldots, a_n$:　variable, subscripted
variable or procedure
identifier

e:　arithmetic or Boolean
expression

RULES:

1.　This statement causes expression "e" to be evaluated and the
result to be assigned to $a_1, a_2, \ldots, a_n$. (Note: there need be
only one variable, e.g., $a_1 \leftarrow e$).

2.　The character "$\leftarrow$" signifies assignment of the value of the
expression to the variables.

3.　The process of assignment is as follows:
a.　Subscripts, if any, occurring in the variables are
evaluated from left to right.
b.　The expression "e" is evaluated.
c.　The value of the expression is assigned to all the variables $a_1, a_2, \ldots, a_n$ from right to left across the left
side.

4. The types of all the variables $a_1, a_2, \ldots, a_n$ must be the same.
   a. If the type is Boolean, the expression "e" must be Boolean.
   b. If the type is real or integer, the expression "e" must be arithmetic.

5. When "e" is an arithmetic expression and its type and the type of the variables is different, the value of "e" is changed to the correct type before it is assigned to a_n. (See Glossary of Terms for forms of integers and real numbers.)

6. In the case in which "e" is real and the variables are integers, "e" is operated upon by the function ENTIER (e+0.5). The result of ENTIER is the largest integer not greater than the value of the argument. This value is then assigned to a_n, etc.

7. The case of a variable being a procedure identifier is only used in defining functions. (See 'PROCEDURE' declaration, function definition.)

EXAMPLES:

In these examples, A, B, C, and D identify 'REAL' type variables. R and S identify 'INTEGER' type variables, and W identifies a 'BOOLEAN' type variable.

1. A←B+C   The value of B + C is assigned to A.

2. A←D←B+C   The value of B + C is
                               assigned to A and D.

3. S←R←3.9   4 is assigned to R and S.

4. A←3.9   3.9 is assigned to A.

5. J←1;   First, 1 is assigned to J.
    S[J]←J←2   Then 2 is assigned to J
                               and S[1].

6. W←A 'GR' B   If the value of A is greater
                               than the value of B, W is
                               assigned the value 'TRUE'
                               otherwise, W is assigned
                               the value 'FALSE'.

PURPOSE: To permit a choice to be made as to which of two expressions is to be evaluated, based on the value of a Boolean expression; to assign the value of the evaluated expression to one or more variables or procedure identifiers.

FORM: $a_1 \leftarrow a_2 \leftarrow \ldots \leftarrow a_n \leftarrow$ 'IF' b 'THEN' e_1 'ELSE' e_2

$a_1, a_2, \ldots, a_n$: variable, subscripted variable or procedure identifier

b: Boolean expression

e_1, e_2: arithmetic or Boolean expression

RULES:

1. Subscripts, if any, occurring in the variables $a_1, a_2, \ldots, a_n$ are evaluated from left to right.

2. The Boolean expression "b" is evaluated.

3. If the value of b is 'TRUE' expression e_1 is evaluated; if 'FALSE' e_2 is evaluated.

4. After e_1 or e_2 is evaluated, this statement operates as a simple assignment statement with the evaluated expression.

EXAMPLES:

1. P←'IF' Q 'LS' 10.0 'THEN' R   *If Q<10, P receives the*
   'ELSE' S + 17.5   *value of R, otherwise S*
                                 +17.5.

2.   A←B←C←'IF' D 'THEN' E
     'OR' F 'ELSE' G 'AND' H

If D is true, the value of E
'OR' F is assigned to A, B
and C. Otherwise, the value
of G 'AND' H is assigned.

Assignment, two
'IF' clauses

PURPOSE: To permit a choice to be made as to which of three expressions
is to be evaluated, based on the values of two Boolean expressions; to assign the value of the evaluated expression to one
or more variables or procedure identifiers.

FORM:
$$a_1 \leftarrow a_2 \leftarrow \ldots \leftarrow a_n \leftarrow \text{'IF'} \; b_1 \; \text{'THEN'} \; e_1 \; \text{'ELSE'} \; \text{'IF'} \; b_2 \; \text{'THEN'} \; e_2 \; \text{'ELSE'} \; e_3$$

$a_1, a_2, \ldots, a_n$: variable, subscripted
variable or procedure
identifier

b_1, b_2: Boolean expression

e_1, e_2, e_3: arithmetic or Boolean
expression

RULES:

1. Subscripts, if any, occurring in the variables $a_1, a_2, \ldots, a_n$
   are evaluated from left to right.

2. The Boolean expression "b_1" is evaluated.

3. If b_1 is true, e_1 is evaluated; if b_1 is false, b_2 is evaluate.

4. If b_2 is true, e_2 is evaluated; if b_2 is false, e_3 is evaluate

5. After an expression is evaluated this statement operates as
   a simple assignment statement with the evaluated expression.

EXAMPLES:

    1. R←'IF' T 'THEN' B-6.2 'ELSE'
       'IF' U 'THEN' C-7 'ELSE' D/3.5

           If T is true R is assigned the value of B-6.2. If T is false and U is true, C-7 is assigned to R. Otherwise, D/3.5 is assigned to R.

Assignment, n
'IF' clauses

PURPOSE: To permit a choice to be made as to which of a number of
expressions is to be evaluated, based on the value of
Boolean expressions; to assign the value of the evaluated
expression to one or more variables or procedure identifiers.

FORM: $a_1 \leftarrow a_2 \leftarrow \ldots \leftarrow a_m \leftarrow$ 'IF' b_1 'THEN' e_1 'ELSE' 'IF'
b_2 'THEN' e_2 'ELSE' ... 'IF' b_n 'THEN' e_n 'ELSE' e_{n+1}

$a_1, a_2, \ldots, a_m$: variable, subscripted
variable or procedure
identifier

$b_1, b_2, \ldots, b_n$: Boolean expression

$e_1, e_2, \ldots, e_{n+1}$: arithmetic or Boolean
expression

RULES:

1. Subscripts, if any, occurring in the variables $a_1, a_2, \ldots, a_n$
are evaluated from left to right.

2. The Boolean expressions $b_1, b_2, \ldots, b_n$ are evaluated from left
to right until one is found which has a value of 'TRUE'.

3. If b_i is found to be true, then e_i is evaluated.

4. If all the Boolean expressions are false, e_{n+1} will be
evaluated.

5. After step 3 or 4 above, this statement operates as a simple
assignment statement with the evaluated expression.

EXAMPLE:

C←D[4,2,2] ← 'IF' B 'OR' E
'THEN' 5 'ELSE' 'IF' T 'THEN' 7.5
'ELSE' 'IF' A 'LS' C 'THEN' G
'ELSE' L

C and D [4,2,2] may be assigned the following values: 5 if either B or E is true; 7.5 if T is true; the value of G if the value of A is less than the value of C; the value of L if none of the above conditions is true.

Conditional Statements

PURPOSE: To permit a statement to be executed or skipped depending
on the value of a Boolean expression.

FORM: 'IF' *b* 'THEN' *s*

                                                    b: Boolean expression
                                                    s: statement

RULES:

1. Statement *s* may be any one of the following:
    a. assignment statement
    b. 'GO TO' statement
    c. dummy statement
    d. 'FOR' statement
    e. procedure statement
    f. compound statement
    g. block

2. Statement *s* may have a label.

3. If the Boolean expression has a value of 'TRUE', statement *s*
    is executed. If *s* does not explicity specify its successor
    the statement following will be executed next.

4. If the Boolean expression has a value of 'FALSE', statement
    s is skipped and the following statement will be executed
    next.

Conditional,
simple

1. 'IF' A 'GR' B 'THEN' D←E*F

    If the value of A is greater than the value of B, then the value of E*F is assigned to D. Otherwise, the assignment statement is skipped and the statement following it is executed.

2. 'IF' L 'THEN' 'BEGIN' P←P+3; R←17.5-T; L←'FALSE' 'END'; 'GO TO' S9

    If L is true the compound statement enclosed between 'BEGIN' and 'END' will be executed; followed by 'GO TO' S9; if L is false only 'GO TO' S9 will be executed.

PURPOSE: *To permit a choice to be made as to which one of two specified statements is to be executed. The decision is based on the value of a Boolean expression.*

FORM: 'IF' b 'THEN' s_1 'ELSE' s_2

b: *Boolean expression*
s_1, s_2:   *statement*

RULES:

1.   *The statements s_1 and s_2 may be any of the following:*
     a.   *assignment statement*
     b.   'GO TO' *statement*
     c.   *procedure statement*
     d.   *dummy statement*
     e.   *compound statement*
     f.   *block*

2.   *Statements s_2 may also be a* 'FOR' *statement.*

3.   *Statements s_1 and s_2 may be labelled.*

4.   *If the Boolean expression has a value of* 'TRUE', *statement s_1 is executed. If s_1 does not explicity specify its successor, then the statement following the conditional statement is executed next, i.e., s_2 is skipped.*

5.   *If the Boolean expression has a value of* 'FALSE', *statement s_2 is executed. If s_2 does not explicity specify its successor the statement following the conditional statement is executed next.*

Conditional, 'ELSE'

EXAMPLES:

1.   'IF' A 'LS' B 'THEN'   *If A is less than B*
   T←T+1 'ELSE' B←B+1;   *T←T+1 is executed, followed*
   'GO TO' L1   *by 'GO TO' L1. If A is*
                                    greater than or equal to B,
                                    B←B+1 is executed, followed
                                    by 'GO TO' L1.

2.   'IF' R 'AND' S 'THEN' 'GO TO'   *If the expression is true,*
   BOB 'ELSE' JOE: M←N+P; 'GO TO'   *control is transferred to*
   BOB   *the statement labelled BOB;*
                                    if false, the statement
                                    labelled JOE is executed
                                    and then control goes to
                                    the statement labelled BOB.

PURPOSE: *To permit a choice to be made as to which of two statements is to be executed or whether neither is to be executed, depending on the value of two Boolean expressions.*

FORM: 'IF' b_1 'THEN' s_1 'ELSE' 'IF' b_2 'THEN' s_2

b_1, b_2:   *Boolean expression*
s_1, s_2:   *statement*

RULES:

1. *Statements s_1 and s_2 may be any one of the following:*
   a. *assignment statement*
   b. *'GO TO' statement*
   c. *dummy statement*
   d. *procedure statement*
   e. *compound statement*
   f. *block*

2. *Statement s_2 may also be a 'FOR' statement.*

3. *Statement s_1 and s_2 may be labelled.*

4. *If b_1 has a value of 'TRUE', statement s_1 is executed. If s_1 does not explicitly specify its successor, the statement following the conditional statement is executed next.*

5. *If b_1 has a value of 'FALSE', b_2 is evaluated.*

6. *If* b_2 *has a value of* 'TRUE', *statement* s_2 *is executed. If* s_2 *does not explicitly specify its successor, the statement following the conditional statement is executed next.*

7. *If* b_2 *has a value of* 'FALSE', *then* s_2 *is skipped and the statement following the complete conditional statement is executed next.*

EXAMPLE:

```
'IF' A 'EQ' B 'THEN' MODE (C,D)
'ELSE' 'IF' A 'GR' B 'THEN' MEAN
(T,D); R←D*F
```

If A=B, *procedure MODE is executed, followed by* R←D*F. *If* A≠B *but* A>B, *then procedure MEAN is executed followed by* R←D*F. *If* A<B, *then only* R←D*F *is executed.*

PURPOSE: To permit a choice to be made as to which of three statements
is to be executed depending upon the value of two Boolean
expressions.

FORM: 'IF' b_1 'THEN' s_1 'ELSE' 'IF' b_2 'THEN' s_2 'ELSE' s_3

b_1, b_2:   Boolean expression

s_1, s_2, s_3:   statement

RULES:

1. Statements s_1, s_2, and s_3 may be any one of the following:
    a. assignment statement
    b. 'GO TO' statement
    c. dummy statement
    d. procedure statement
    e. compound statement
    f. block

2. Statement s_3 may also be a 'FOR' statement.

3. Statements s_1, s_2, and s_3 may be labelled.

4. If b_1 has a value of 'TRUE', statement s_1 is executed. If
    s_1 does not explicitly specify its successor, the statement
    following the conditional statement is executed next.

5. If b_1 is false, b_2 is evaluated.

51

6. *If b_2 has a value of* 'TRUE', *statement s_2 is executed. If s_2 does not explicitly specify its successor, the statement following the conditional statement is executed next.*

7. *If b_2 has a value of* 'FALSE', *statement s_3 is executed. If s_3 does not explicitly specify its successor, the statement following the conditional statement is executed next.*

EXAMPLE:

```
'IF' L 'THEN' 'GO TO' BOY 'ELSE'
'IF' R 'GR' S 'THEN' 'BEGIN'
A←A+1; CALC (F,10) 'END' 'ELSE'
'GO TO' CAT; R←R+1
```

If L is true, control goes to the statement labelled BOY; if L is false, R is compared to S; if R>S, the compound statement is executed followed by R←R+1. If R≤S, control goes to the statement labelled CAT.

PURPOSE: To permit *a choice* to be made among a number of statements
as which one should be executed, or whether none is to be
executed, depending upon the value of Boolean expressions.

FORM:

$$\text{'IF' } b_1 \text{ 'THEN' } s_1 \text{ 'ELSE' 'IF' } b_2 \text{ 'THEN' } s_2 \text{ 'ELSE' } \ldots$$
$$\text{'IF' } b_{n-1} \text{ 'THEN' } s_{n-1} \text{ 'ELSE' 'IF' } b_n \text{ 'THEN' } s_n$$

$$b_1, b_2, \ldots, b_n: \quad \text{Boolean expression}$$
$$s_1, s_2, \ldots, s_n: \quad \text{statement}$$

RULES:

1. Each statement $s_1, s_2, \ldots, s_n$ may be any one of the following:
    a. assignment statement
    b. 'GO TO' statement
    c. dummy statement
    d. procedure statement
    e. compound statement
    f. block

2. Statement s_n may be a 'FOR' statement.

3. Statements $s_1, s_2, \ldots, s_n$ may be labelled.

4. The Boolean expressions are evaluated in the order $b_1, b_2, \ldots,$
    until one having a value of 'TRUE' is found. If b_i is true,
    statement s_i is executed. If statement s_i does not explicitly
    specify its successor, the statement following the conditional
    statement is executed next.

5. If none of the Boolean expressions is true, the statement
    following the complete conditional statement is executed
    next.

Conditional, n
'IF' clauses

```
'IF' M 'THEN' A←A+1 'ELSE'
'IF' N 'THEN' 'GO TO' R1 'ELSE'
'IF' P 'THEN'
'FOR' I←1 'STEP' 1 'UNTIL' 10 'DO'
A[I] ←I; L←M 'OR' P
```

*If M is true, the value of
A is increased by 1. If M
is false and N is true, then
'GO TO' R1 is executed. If
M and N are false and P is
true, the 'FOR' statement
is executed. If M, N and P
are all false, the statement
L←M 'OR' P is executed.*

PURPOSE: To permit a choice to be made among a number of statements as to which one should be executed depending upon the value of Boolean expressions.

FORM: 'IF' b_1 'THEN' s_1 'ELSE' 'IF' b_2 'THEN' s_2 'ELSE' ...
'IF' b_{n-1} 'THEN' s_{n-1} 'ELSE' s_n

$b_1, b_2, \ldots, b_{n-1}$: Boolean expression
$s_1, s_2, \ldots, s_n$: statement

RULES:

1. Each statement $s_1, s_2, \ldots, s_n$ may be any one of the following:
    a. assignment statement
    b. 'GO TO' statement
    c. dummy statement
    d. procedure statement
    e. compound statement
    f. block

2. Statement s_n may be a 'FOR' statement.

3. Statements $s_1, s_2, \ldots, s_n$ may be labelled.

4. The Boolean expressions are evaluated in the order $b_1, b_2, \ldots,$ until one having a value of 'TRUE' is found. If b_i is true, statement s_i is executed. If statement s_i does not explicitly specify its successor, the statement following the complete conditional statement is executed next.

5. If none of the Boolean expressions is true, statement s_n
    will be executed. If it does not explicitly specify its
    successor, the statement following the conditional state-
    ment is executed next.

EXAMPLE:

```
'IF' A 'THEN' I←I+1 'ELSE'
'IF' B 'THEN' J←J+1 'ELSE'
'IF' C 'THEN' K←K+1 'ELSE'
L←L+1;
'IF' D 'THEN' 'GO TO' BAD
```

If A is true, the value of
I is increased by one. If
A is false and B is true,
the value of J is increased
by one. If A and B are false
and C is true, the value of
K is increased by one. If
A, B and C are false, the
value of L is increased by
one. If D is true then
'GO TO' BAD is executed.
Otherwise, the statement
following it is executed.

Dummy Statement

PURPOSE: *To place a label at a particular point in the program.*

FORM: *(null form)*

RULES:

    1.   This statement causes no operation.

EXAMPLES:

    1.   `COUNT:;`   *COUNT is the label of a dummy statement.*

    2.   `B3: ; ABC:`   *B3 is the label of a dummy statement.*
        `E←E+1`

    3.   `'BEGIN'...;`   *TOY is the label of a dummy statement.*
        `TOY: 'END'`

'FOR' *Statements*

PURPOSE: To permit a statement to be executed for a specified value
of a controlled variable.

FORM: 'FOR' v←e 'DO' s

> v: variable or subscripted
> variable
> e: arithmetic expression
> s: statement

RULES:

1. Variable v is called the controlled variable of the 'FOR'
statement.

2. e represents a value which is assigned to v.

3. Statement s may be a simple statement, a compound statement
or a block.

4. The 'FOR' statement causes the expression e to be evaluated
and its value assigned to v. Then statement s is executed.

5. After statement s is executed with v having the value of e,
the 'FOR' statement has been executed. If s does not explicitly
specify its successor, the statement following the 'FOR' statement is executed next.

6. After execution of the 'FOR' statement, the value of v is
undefined.

'FOR', *expression*

7. *If control is transferred from the* 'FOR' *statement by a statement (within statement s), the value of v is available.*

8. *A* 'GO TO' *statement outside the* 'FOR' *statement may not refer to a label within the* 'FOR' *statement.*

EXAMPLES:

1. `'FOR' J←I 'DO' A[J]←0.0`

    This statement causes zero to be assigned to location A[I].

2. `'FOR' R←2*BOY↑ 2 'DO'`
    `'BEGIN' T←T+1; B[R]← -C[R]`
    `'END'`

    This statement results in -C[2* BOY↑ 2] assigned to B[2*BOY↑ 2]. Also, the value of T is increased by one.

PURPOSE: To permit a statement to be executed repeatedly for a specified initial value, increment and final value of a controlled variable.

FORM: 'FOR' $v \leftarrow e_1$ 'STEP' e_2 'UNTIL' e_3 'DO' s

v: variable or subscripted variable

e_1, e_2, e_3:   arithmetic expression

s: statement

RULES:

1. Variable v is called the controlled variable of the 'FOR' statement.

2. e_1 represents the initial value for v; e_2 is the increment of v; e_3 is the final value for v.

3. Statement s may be a simple statement, a compound statement or a block.

4. The first step in the operation of the 'FOR' statement is that v is assigned the value of e_1.

5. Statement s may be executed a number of times as follows:

   a. A test is made to see if the value of v is beyond the bound specified by e_3. If it is, statement s will not be executed. The statement after s is executed next and the value of v is undefined.

     b.   *If v is within the bound, statement s is executed.*

     c.   *If s does not explicitly specify its successor, the value e_2 is then added to v (i.e., $v \leftarrow v + e_2$). If the value of e_2 is positive, this will have the effect of increasing v. If the value of e_2 is negative, v will be reduced. The process is then repeated at step a.*

6.   *If control is transferred from the 'FOR' statement by a statement (within statement s), the value of v is available.*

7.   *The value of the controlled variable, the increment and the final value may be changed by statement s. Therefore, they are evaluated every time reference is made to them.*

8.   *A 'GO TO' statement outside a 'FOR' statement may not refer to a label within the 'FOR' statement.*

EXAMPLES:

1.   `'FOR' I←1 'STEP' 1 'UNTIL' 10 'DO' A[I]←B[I]`   *These statements cause B[1] to B[10] to be assigned to A[1] to A[10].*

2.   `'FOR' K←9 'STEP' −2 'UNTIL' 5 'DO' X[K]←K↑2`   *These statements cause 81 to be assigned to X[9], 49 to be assigned to X[7], and 25 to be assigned to X[5].*

3.  ```
    'FOR' L←1 'STEP' 1 'UNTIL' 5
    'DO'
    'FOR' A[I]←6 'STEP' 1 'UNTIL'
    10 'DO' B[A[L],L]←L
    ```

The order of assignments
caused by these statements
is as follows:
6 to 10 is assigned to A[1]
as 1 is assigned to B[6,1]
      to B[10,1],
6 to 10 is assigned to A[2]
as 2 is assigned to B[6,2]
      to B[10,2], etc.
Finally,
6 to 10 is assigned to A[5]
as 5 is assigned to B[6,5]
      to B[10,5].
    ```

'FOR', 'WHILE'
clause

PURPOSE: *To permit a statement to be executed repeatedly for assigned values of a controlled variable with repetition controlled by the value of a Boolean expression.*

FORM: `'FOR'` $v \leftarrow e$ `'WHILE'` b `'DO'` s

v: *variable or subscripted variable*
e: *arithmetic expression*
b: *Boolean expression*
s: *statement*

RULES:

1. *Variable v is called the controlled variable of the* `'FOR'` *statement.*

2. *Statement s may be a simple statement, a compound statement or a block.*

3. *This statement causes statement s to be executed repeatedly as long as the value of the Boolean expression b is true.*

4. *This statement operates as follows:*
   a. *e is evaluated and its value is assigned to v.*
   b. *The Boolean expression b is evaluated.*
   c. *If b is true, statement s is executed. If s does not explicitly specify its successor, the process is repeated at step a.*
   d. *If b is false, statement s is not executed and the statement following statement s is executed next. The value of v is undefined in this case.*

5. If control is transferred from the 'FOR' statement by a 'GO TO' statement (within statement s), the value of v is available.

6. The values of either e or b may be changed by statement s.

7. A 'GO TO' statement outside a 'FOR' statement may not refer to a label within the 'FOR' statement.

EXAMPLE:

```
J←1;
'FOR' I←J 'WHILE' I 'LS' 10 'DO'
'BEGIN'
   A[I]←I;
   J←J+1
'END'
```

These statements cause 1 to 9 to be assigned to A[1] to A[9].

'FOR',
general

PURPOSE: *To permit a statement to be executed repeatedly for various conditions governing a controlled variable.*

FORM: 'FOR' $v \leftarrow a_1, a_2, \ldots, a_n$ 'DO' s

> v: *variable or subscripted variable*
>
> $a_1, a_2, \ldots, a_n$: *arithmetic expression, 'STEP' clause, or 'WHILE' clause*
>
> s: *statement*

RULES:

1. *Variable v is called the controlled variable of the 'FOR' statement.*

2. *$a_1, a_2, \ldots, a_n$ may be any combination of arithmetic expressions, 'STEP' clauses, or 'WHILE' clauses.*

3. *s may be a simple statement, a compound statement or a block.*

4. *If a_i is an arithmetic expression, a 'STEP' clause or a 'WHILE' clause, the 'FOR' statement operates as previously described. The order of operation is $a_1, a_2, \ldots, a_n$.*

EXAMPLE:
```
'FOR' X←3, 2 'STEP' 1 'UNTIL' 5,
70, 60, A 'WHILE' Z, 80 'DO'
P(X)
```

First, 3 is assigned to X and procedure P(X) is executed.

Then the 'STEP' clause causes the following action: 2 is assigned to X and P(X) is executed. X is stepped by 1 three times causing it to assume the values 3, 4 and 5. P(X) is executed after each step of X. Next, X is assigned the value 70, and P(X) is executed.

Then X is assigned the value 60, and P(X) is executed.

The 'WHILE' clause causes the value of A to be assigned to X. If Z is true, P(X) is executed. This is repeated until Z becomes false. (The values of A and Z may be changed by execution of P(X)).

Finally, 80 is assigned to X and P(X) is executed.

71

'GO TO' *Statements*

PURPOSE: To interrupt the normal sequence of statement execution by
defining explicitly the successor of the current statement.

FORM: 'GO TO' a

a: statement label

RULES:

1. The statement 'GO TO' a causes control to go to the statement
with label a.

2. A 'GO TO' statement outside a 'FOR' statement may not refer
to a label within the 'FOR' statement.

3. A 'GO TO' statement outside a block may not refer to a label
within that block.

4. A 'GO TO' statement outside a compound statement may refer
to label within that compound statement.

EXAMPLES:

1. 'GO TO' BOY

    This statement causes control to go to a statement labelled BOY.

2. 'GO TO' T12; M15: A←A+1;
    'IF' L 'THEN' 'BEGIN' C←D*E↑2;
    T12: A←B+C*F 'END'

    The 'GO TO' statement causes control to go to a statement within a compound statement.

'GO TO',
switch designator

PURPOSE: *To interrupt the normal sequence of statement execution by causing control to be transferred to one of a number of possible statements depending on the value of an arithmetic expression.*

FORM: 'GO TO' *sw* [*a*]

sw: switch identifier
a: arithmetic expression

RULES:

1. *The switch identifier "sw" must have been defined by a switch declaration in the current block or in an enclosing block.*

2. *The form sw [a] is called a switch designator.*

3. *The next statement to be executed is the one whose label is referenced through the switch declaration defining "sw".*

4. *This* 'GO TO' *statement operates as follows:*
    a. *The expression denoted by a is evaluated. From this value an integer k is established where k is the result of the function* ENTIER *(a+0.5). That is, the largest integer not greater than the value of the argument, i.e., if a is 3.7, k=4.*
    b. *k specifies which element in the list of the switch declaration will be referenced, i.e., the leftmost element is numbered 1; the next is 2, etc.*

   c.   *If k is not within the range 1 to n (where n is the*
       number of elements in the switch designator), control
       goes to the next statement in normal sequence.

5.   *A 'GO TO' statement outside a 'FOR' statement may not refer*
    to a label within that 'FOR' statement.

6.   *A 'GO TO' statement outside a block may not refer to a label*
    within that block.

7.   *A 'GO TO' statement outside a compound statement may refer to*
    a label within that compound statement.

EXAMPLE:

```
'BEGIN'
'SWITCH' AB←PB, QB;
'SWITCH' AC←PC, QC, AB[X];
 ...
'GO TO' AB[T];
 ...
'GO TO' AC[Y];
 ...
'END'
```

If T has the value 1 when the 'GO TO' for switch AB is executed, control goes to the statement labelled PB. If T has the value 2, control goes to the statement labelled QB. If T has any other value, control goes to the statement following the 'GO TO' statement. When the 'GO TO' for switch AC is executed, control will go to statements labelled PC or QC if Y has the value one or two, respectively. If Y has the value three, then execution is equivalent to 'GO TO' AB[X]. If Y has any other value, control goes to the next sequential statement.

'GO TO',
conditional designator

PURPOSE: To interrupt the normal sequence of statement execution by
causing control to be transferred to one of a number of
possible statements; the statement chosen will depend on
the value of a Boolean expression.

FORM: 'GO TO' 'IF' b 'THEN' d_1 'ELSE' d_2

b: Boolean expression

d_1, d_2 designational expression

RULES:

1. A designational expression (d_1, d_2) is any one of the following:
   a. Statement label
   b. Switch designator. This has the form $sw[a]$, where sw
       represents a switch identifier and a represents an
       arithmetic expression.
   c. Conditional designator. This has the form
           'IF' b 'THEN' c 'ELSE' d
       where b represents a Boolean expression;
           c may be either a statement label, a switch designator,
           or a conditional designator enclosed within
           parentheses;
           d may be either a statement label, a switch designator,
           or a conditional designator (not necessarily enclosed
           within parentheses).

2. This statement operates as follows:
   a. The Boolean expression b is evaluated;
   b. If b is true, control is transferred as specified by d_1;

c. If the Boolean expression b is false, control is transferred as specified by d_2.

3. A 'GO TO' statement outside a 'FOR' statement may not refer to a label within that 'FOR' statement.

4. A 'GO TO' statement outside a compound statement may refer to a label within that compound statement.

EXAMPLES:

1. 'GO TO' 'IF' A 'THEN' B 'ELSE' C[I]

    If the Boolean expression A is true, control goes to the statement labelled B. Otherwise, control goes to the statement referenced by the Ith item in the switch declaration defining C.

2. 'GO TO' 'IF' BA 'THEN' LA 'ELSE' 'IF' BB 'THEN' LB 'ELSE' LC

    If the Boolean expression BA is true, control goes to the statement labelled LA. If expression BA is false and Boolean expression BB is true, control goes to the statement labelled LB. If both expressions BA and BB are false, control goes to the statement labelled LC. (Note: d_1 in this case is a statement label while d_2 is a conditional designator.)

3. 'GO TO' 'IF' BA 'THEN' ('IF' BB 'THEN' LB 'ELSE' LC) 'ELSE' LA

If both BA and BB are true, control goes to the statement labelled LB. If BA is true and BB is false, control goes to the statement labelled LC. If BA is false, control goes to the statement labelled LA. (Note: d_1 is a conditional designator and, therefore, must be enclosed in parentheses.)

Procedure Statement

PURPOSE: To call for the execution of a procedure defined by a
                 'PROCEDURE' *declaration.*

FORM: (1)   name

                 (2)   name $(a_1 \ t \ a_2 \ t \ \ldots \ t \ a_n)$

$$\begin{aligned} name: &\quad procedure \ identifier \\ a_1, a_2, \ldots, a_n: &\quad actual \ parameter \\ t: &\quad separator \end{aligned}$$

RULES:

1.   A procedure statement may have no parameters as shown in
     FORM (1).

2.   When there are parameters (FORM (2)), each separator t may be
     either "," or ")b:(" where b represents any sequence of letters.
     The function of b is only descriptive, i.e., it may be used
     as comments to describe actual parameters. b has no operational
     significance.

3.   The procedure identifier must appear in a procedure declaration.

4.   The number of actual parameters must be the same as the number
     of formal parameters in the procedure declaration. However,
     the method of parameter separation need not be the same in a
     procedure statement and the corresponding declaration. That
     is, where a comma was used in a procedure statement, the form
     ")b:(" may be used in the declaration and vice versa.

5. The actual parameters may be any one of the following:
   a. arithmetic expression
   b. Boolean expression
   c. string
   d. array identifier
   e. switch identifier
   f. procedure identifier
   g. designational expression

6. The correspondence between the actual parameters of the procedure statement and the formal parameters of the procedure declaration is by their appearance in the respective parameter lists. The two sets of parameters must have the same number of items.

7. The execution of a procedure statement is as follows:
   a. The formal parameters which appear in a value list of the procedure declaration are replaced by the values of the corresponding actual parameters.
   b. These actual parameters are evaluated from left to right according to their appearance in the parameter list.
   c. Formal parameters which are not part of a value list are replaced throughout the procedure by the corresponding actual parameters.
   d. If the identifier of an actual parameter and an identifier already in the procedure are the same, adjustments will automatically be made to the latter so that no conflicts occur.
   e. After the procedure has been modified as above, it is executed.

8. If an actual parameter is a string, it may only be used in a procedure written in non-ALGOL code. In an ALGOL procedure, a string may appear only as an actual parameter for a further procedure call.

9. An actual parameter corresponding to a formal parameter which appears on the left side of an assignment statement in the procedure must be a variable or a subscripted variable.

10. If a formal parameter is an array identifier, the corresponding actual parameter must also be an array identifier of the same dimension.

11. A switch identifier or string may not be an actual parameter corresponding to a formal parameter which is called by value. A procedure identifier may not be used as a value parameter unless it designates a function with no arguments.

EXAMPLES:

1. HIGHVAL (Z, P*(P+1)/2 , V, I)   The procedure which this statement calls is defined in the section 'PROCEDURE' declaration, simple. In this procedure statement Z denotes the number of elements. The value of the largest element of Z will be found in V after the procedure call, and I will contain the value of the subscript of the largest element.

2. SQUAREROOT (A↑2+B↑2, .000001, C)

The procedure which this statement calls is defined in the section 'PROCEDURE' declaration, specification part. After this procedure statement is executed, C will contain the square root of A^2+B^2 with an accuracy of .000001.

3. TOT (X, A, 1, N, 1/A✕(A+1))

The procedure which this statement calls is defined in the section 'PROCEDURE' declaration, value and specification part. This procedure statement will result in the following computation:

$$X = \sum_{A=1}^{N} 1/A(A+1)$$

4. SUM←ADD (A, I, N) FUNCTION:
    (1/A✕(A+1))

The procedure which this statement calls is defined in the section 'PROCEDURE' declaration, function definition. This function call will result in the summation of example 3 in ADD and in SUM. The symbol FUNCTION is used as text and has no operational significance.

5. SUM←ADD(P,Q,N⋇(N+1),
    ADD(Q,1,N,P/Q))

This statement results in the value of the following computation placed in ADD and in SUM:

$$\sum_{P=Q}^{N(N+1)} \quad \sum_{Q=1}^{N} \; P/Q$$

This is an example of a recursive procedure call.

IV. *Declarations*

'ARRAY' *Declarations*

PURPOSE: To specify array identifiers, dimensions, bounds of subscripts
and their types.

FORM: type 'ARRAY' $a_1, a_2, \ldots, a_n$

type: type word
$a_1, a_2, \ldots, a_n$: array specifier

RULES:

1. The type word may be any one of the following:
   a. 'INTEGER'
   b. 'REAL'
   c. 'BOOLEAN'

2. Type is optional. If it is not used, 'REAL' is assumed.
   The type is assigned to each array identifier in the
   declaration.

3. An array specifier may be either of the form b or b[c], where
   b represents an array identifier and c represents a dimension
   specifier. A dimension specifier has the form $d_1: e_1, d_2: e_2, \ldots,$
   $d_n: e_n$, where each d_i and e_i may be an arithmetic expression.
   n is the number of dimensions. d_i and e_i represent the lower
   and upper subscript bounds of dimension i, respectively. The
   value of a lower bound may not exceed the value of an upper
   bound.

4. *If an array identifier does not have a dimension specifier, the next dimension specifier is assigned. That is, the form $b_1, b_2, \ldots, b_m\ [d_1: e_1,\ d_2: e_2, \ldots, d_n: e_n]$ is equivalent to the form $b_1\ [d_1: e_1,\ d_2: e_2, \ldots, d_n: e_n],\ b_2\ [d_1: e_1,\ d_2: e_2, \ldots, d_n: e_n], \ldots; b_m\ [d_1: e_1, d_2: e_2, \ldots, d_n: e_n].$*

5. *Lower and upper bounds will be evaluated from left to right. The bounds can only depend on variables and procedures which have been defined in a block enclosing the block for which the array declaration is valid. Consequently, in the outermost block of a program, only array declarations with constant bounds may be used.*

6. *The bounds will be evaluated each time the block is entered.*

7. *Every array used in a program must appear in an array declaration.*

8. *An array identifier may not appear with subscripts whose values do not lie within the bounds specified by the array declaration.*

EXAMPLES:

1. 'ARRAY' A[1:10] *The array A is one-dimensional and has a lower subscript bound of 1 and an upper subscript bound of 10. A is assumed to be of* 'REAL' *type.*

94

2. 'ARRAY' A,B [1:10,1:20]

Arrays A and B are two
dimensional and have sub-
script bounds 1 and 10 and
1 and 20. The arrays are
assumed to be 'REAL' type.

3. 'INTEGER' 'ARRAY' A[P:Q],
    B [1:2*P, 3:5, 1:5]

The array A is of 'INTEGER'
type and has subscript bounds
P and Q. B is of 'INTEGER'
type and is three dimensional.
The bounds of the dimensions
and 1 and 2*P, 3 and 5, and
1 and 5 respectively.

'ARRAY',
'OWN'

PURPOSE: *To specify array identifiers, dimensions, bounds of subscripts and array types; also to specify the condition of arrays upon re-entry into a block.*

FORM: 'OWN' *type* 'ARRAY' $a_1, a_2, \ldots, a_n$

$$\text{type: } \textit{type word}$$
$$a_1, a_2, \ldots, a_n: \textit{ array specifier}$$

RULES:

1. *The array specifiers may be in any of the forms permissible for the array declaration.*

2. *All the Rules which pertain to array declarations are valid for the* 'OWN' *array declaration except:*
   a. *On re-entry into the block in which the* 'OWN' *array declaration appears the array elements will have their previous values.*
   b. *The subscript bounds must be integer constants.*

3. *When exit is made from the block (by* 'END' *or by a* 'GO TO' *statement), the identifiers are inaccessible even though their values have been saved.*

EXAMPLE:

'OWN' 'BOOLEAN' 'ARRAY'
BA[1:20, 5:15, 1:10]

The array BA is three dimensional and is of 'BOOLEAN' *type. The bounds of the dimensions are 1 and 20, 5 and 15, and 1 and 10, respectively.*

'PROCEDURE' *Declarations*

PURPOSE: *To define a statement or series of statements as being asso-*
ciated with a procedure identifier; to provide a means by
which a procedure may be executed any number of times in the
course of a program although the steps of the procedure appear
only once.

FORM: 1)   'PROCEDURE' *name; s*
           2)   'PROCEDURE' *name* $(a_1 \ t \ a_2 \ t \ ... \ t \ a_n); \ s$

$$name: \quad procedure \ identifier$$
$$a_1, a_2, ..., a_n: \quad formal \ parameter$$
$$t: \quad separator$$
$$s: \quad statement$$

RULES:

1. *A procedure declaration may have no parameters as shown in*
    FORM (1).

2. *When there are parameters (FORM (2)), each separator t may be*
    either "," *or* ")b:(" *where b represents any sequence of*
    letters. The function of b is only descriptive, i.e., it may
    be used as comments to describe actual parameters. b has no
    operational significance.

3. *The formal parameters may be any of the following:*
    a. *variable*
    b. *array identifier*
    c. *switch identifier*
    d. *label*
    e. *procedure identifier*

4. The formal parameters usually appear somewhere in statement s. They will be replaced by or assigned the value of the actual parameters of the particular procedure statement which calls the procedure.

5. Statement s may be
   a. a simple statement
   b. a compound statement
   c. a block

6. Identifiers which are not formal parameters may appear in s if either of the following conditions exists:
   a. s is in the form of a block and the identifiers are declared at the beginning of this block.
   b. the identifiers are declared in the block in which the procedure declaration appears.

7. Statement s always acts like a block insofar as the scope of its identifiers is concerned, i.e., a label appearing in s is not defined outside the procedure declaration.

8. The procedure specified may be executed anywhere in the block in which the declaration appears by writing a procedure statement containing the procedure identifier and the actual parameters, if any.

EXAMPLE:

```
'PROCEDURE' HIGHVAL (A,N) ANS:(X,Y);
   'BEGIN'
      X←A[1]; Y←1;
        'FOR' I←2'STEP' 1 'UNTIL' N 'DO'
        'IF' A[I] 'GR' X 'THEN'
            'BEGIN'
               X←A[I]; Y←I
            'END'
   'END'
```

This procedure determines the largest element of an array. Input formal parameters are: array identifier A and number N of elements. Output formal parameters are: value X of largest element and value Y of subscript of largest element. The symbol ANS is used as text and has no operational significance.

'PROCEDURE' *declaration,*
specification part

PURPOSE: *To define a statement or series of statements as being associated with a procedure identifier; to provide a means by which a procedure may be executed any number of times in the course of a program although the steps of the procedure appear only once; to specify the kinds of quantities actual parameters may represent.*

FORM:

$$\text{'PROCEDURE'} \; name \; (a_1 \; t \; a_2 \; t \; \ldots \; t \; a_n)$$
$$sp \; list; \; sp \; list; \ldots; \; sp \; list; \; s$$

name:	*procedure identifier*
$a_1, a_2, \ldots, a_n$:	*formal parameter*
t:	*separator*
sp:	*specifier*
list:	*formal parameters separated by commas*
s:	*statement*

RULES:

1. *Each separator t may be either "," or ")b:(" where b represents any sequence of letters. The function of b is only descriptive, i.e., it may be used as comments to describe actual parameters. b has no operational significance.*

2. *The formal parameters may be any of the following:*
    a. *variable*
    b. *array identifier*
    c. *label*
    d. *switch identifier*
    e. *procedure identifier*

3. *The formal parameters usually appear somewhere in statement s. They are replaced at the time of execution by the actual parameters of the procedure statement.*

4. *The specifiers may be any of the following:*

'ARRAY'	'INTEGER' 'ARRAY'
'BOOLEAN'	'INTEGER' 'PROCEDURE'
'BOOLEAN' 'ARRAY'	'LABEL'
'BOOLEAN' 'PROCEDURE'	'PROCEDURE'
'INTEGER'	'REAL'
	'REAL' 'ARRAY'
	'REAL' 'PROCEDURE'
	'STRING'
	'SWITCH'

5. *The specifiers indicate for the parameters in their "list" what form the corresponding actual parameters should take. (Note: 'INTEGER' and 'REAL' may be used interchangeably and the proper transformations will take place automatically.)*

6. *A formal parameter may appear in no more than one "list." However, a formal parameter need not appear in a "list," except for switches which must be specified.*

7. *Statement s may be*
   a. *a simple statement*
   b. *a compound statement*
   c. *a block*

8. *Identifiers which are not formal parameters may appear in
   s if either of the following conditions exists:*
   a. *s is a block and the identifiers are declared at the
      beginning of this block.*
   b. *the identifiers are declared in the block in which the
      procedure declaration appears.*

9. *Statement s always acts like a block insofar as the scope of
   its identifiers is concerned, i.e., a label appearing in s
   is not defined outside the procedure declaration.*

10. *The procedure specified may be executed anywhere in the block
    in which the declaration appears by writing a procedure state-
    ment containing the procedure identifier and the actual
    parameters.*

EXAMPLE:

```
'PROCEDURE' SQUAREROOT (X,E,S);
'REAL' X, E, S;
'BEGIN' 'REAL' SA;
   'IF' X 'LS' 0 'THEN'
   'BEGIN' S←-1; 'GO TO' B 'END';
   SA←1;
   A: S←(SA+X/SA)/2;
   'IF' ABS(SA-S) 'GR' E 'THEN'
      'BEGIN' SA←S; 'GO TO' A 'END';
B: 'END'
```

*This procedure computes
the square root. Input
formal parameters are:
number X whose square root
is wanted and accuracy E.
Output formal parameter is
square root S of X.*

PURPOSE: To define a statement or series of statements as being associated with a procedure identifier; to provide a means by
which a procedure may be executed any number of times in
the course of a program although the steps of the procedure
appear only once; to specify which formal parameters are
replaced by the value of the corresponding actual parameters;
to specify the kinds of quantities actual parameters may
represent.

FORM: 'PROCEDURE' *name* $(a_1 \ t \ a_2 \ t \ ... \ t \ a_n)$
            'VALUE' *list;*
            sp list; sp list;...; sp list, s

name:	procedure identifier
$a_1, a_2, ..., a_n:$	formal parameter
t:	separator
sp:	specifier
s:	statement
list:	formal parameters sepa-rated by commas

RULES:

1. Each separator t may be either "," or ")b:(" where b repre-
    sents any sequence of letters. The function of b is only
    descriptive, i.e., it may be used as comments to describe
    actual parameters. b has no operational significance.

'PROCEDURE' declaration,
value and specification
part

2. The formal parameters may be any of the following:
   a. variable
   b. array identifier
   c. label
   d. switch identifier
   e. procedure identifier

3. The formal parameters usually appear somewhere in statement s. They are replaced at the time the procedure is called upon by the actual parameters of the procedure statement.

4. However, those formal parameters which are listed in the 'VALUE' part of the declaration are assigned the current values of the corresponding actual parameters before statement s is executed. The order of assignment is from left to right according to the order of appearance in the formal parameter list.

5. The specifier may be any of the following:

   'ARRAY'   'INTEGER' 'ARRAY'
   'BOOLEAN'   'INTEGER' 'PROCEDURE'
   'BOOLEAN' 'ARRAY'   'LABEL'
   'BOOLEAN' 'PROCEDURE'   'PROCEDURE'
   'INTEGER'   'REAL'
                                'REAL' 'ARRAY'
                                'REAL' 'PROCEDURE'
                                'STRING'
                                'SWITCH'

6. The specifiers indicate, for the parameters in their list, what form the corresponding actual parameters should take. (Note: 'INTEGER' and 'REAL' and may be used interchangeably and the proper transformations will be made automatically.)

7. A formal parameter may appear in no more than one specification
    list. However, a formal parameter need not appear in a list,
    except for switches which must be specified.

8. A formal parameter appearing in the 'VALUE' list must also
    appear in one of the specification lists.

9. Statement s may be:
    a. a simple statement
    b. a compound statement
    c. a block

10. Identifiers which are not formal parameters may appear in s
     if either of the following conditions exists:
     a. s is a block and the identifiers are declared at the
         beginning of this block.
     b. the identifiers are declared in the block in which the
         procedure declaration appears.

11. Statement s always acts like a block insofar as the scope of
     its identifiers is concerned, i.e., a label appearing in s is
     not defined outside the procedure declaration.

12. The procedure specified may be executed anywhere in the block
     in which the declaration appears by writing a procedure state-
     ment containing the procedure identifier and the actual para-
     meters.

'PROCEDURE' declaration, value and specification part

EXAMPLE:

```
'PROCEDURE' TOT(T,K,L,M,U);
'VALUE' L,M; 'INTEGER' L,M;
'BEGIN'
   T←0;
    'FOR' K←L 'STEP' 1 'UNTIL' M 'DO'
   T←T+U
'END'
```

This procedure computes the sum of values of a function U between the limits of summation L and M. The function U may depend on the summation index K. The sum is generated in formal parameter T.

'PROCEDURE' *declaration, function definition*

PURPOSE: To define a statement or series of statements associated with a specific procedure identifier as being a function; to provide a means by which the appearance of the procedure identifier will cause the function to be performed and a value to be given to the identifier although the steps of the function appear only once.

FORM:

(1)   type 'PROCEDURE' name; s

(2)   type 'PROCEDURE' name (a_1 t a_2 t ... t a_n); s

(3)   type 'PROCEDURE' name (a_1 t a_2 t ... t a_n);
    sp list; sp list;...; sp list; s

(4)   type 'PROCEDURE' name (a_1 t a_2 t ... t a_n);
    'VALUE' list;
    sp list; sp list;...; sp list; s

type:	type word
name:	procedure identifier
$a_1, a_2, ..., a_n$:	formal parameter
t:	separator
sp:	specifier
s:	statement
list:	formal parameters separated by commas

RULES:

1. A procedure declaration may have no parameters as shown in FORM (1).

2. When there are parameters (FORM (2), (3), (4)),each separator t may be either "," or ")b:(" where b represents any sequence of letters. The function of b is only descriptive, i.e., it may be used as comments to describe actual parameters. b has no operational significance.

3. The type word may be any of the following:
   a. 'INTEGER'
   b. 'BOOLEAN'
   c. 'REAL'
   The type word identifies the type of the procedure identifier.

4. At some point in the procedure body, i.e., in statement s, the procedure identifier must appear on the left side of an assignment statement. When this statement is executed, the function receives a value, and it is this value which is used when the procedure identifier appears in an expression. The function receives a value according to the type specified by the type word.

5. The procedure identifier may appear on the left side of any number of assignment statements. It is the last one to be executed from which the function receives its value.

6. The formal parameters may be any of the following:
   a. variable
   b. array identifier
   c. label
   d. switch identifier
   e. procedure identifier

7. The formal parameters usually appear in statement s. They are replaced at the time the procedure is called upon by the actual parameters of the function call.

8. There may or may not be a 'VALUE' declaration in a function definition. If there is, the rules which apply are the same for all procedure declarations.

9. The specifiers which may be included, and the rules which apply are the same for all procedure declarations.

10. Statement s may be
   a. a simple statement
   b. a compound statement
   c. a block

11. Identifiers which are not formal parameters may appear in s if either of the following conditions exists:
   a. s is a block and the identifiers are declared at the beginning of this block.
   b. the identifiers are declared in the block in which the procedure declaration appears.

12. Statement s always acts like a block insofar as the scope of its identifiers is concerned, i.e., a label appearing in s is not defined outside the procedure declaration.

13. The function which this declaration defines may be executed anywhere in the block in which this declaration appears by writing in an arithemetic or Boolean expression the procedure identifier and the actual parameters, if any.

'PROCEDURE' declaration,
function definition

1.  ```
    'REAL' 'PROCEDURE' ADD(K,L,M,U);
    'BEGIN' 'REAL' W;
       W←0;
        'FOR' K←L 'STEP' 1 'UNTIL' M
        'DO'
               W←W+U;
               ADD←W
    'END'
    ```
    This function computes the sum of values of a function U between the limits of summation L and M. The function U may depend on the summation index K. Upon exit from the function, the sum is contained in ADD which is of type 'REAL'.

2.  ```
    'INTEGER' 'PROCEDURE' FACT(X);
    'IF' X 'EQ' 1 'THEN' FACT←1 'ELSE'
        FACT←X* FACT(X-1)
    ```
    This is an example of a recursive procedure declaration. Execution of FACT(2) causes FACT(1) to be executed because of the statement FACT←2 FACT(1). Then FACT will have the value 2*1. Execution of FACT(3) causes FACT to have the value 3*2*1. If this procedure is called n times, FACT will have the value n factorial.*

'SWITCH' *Declaration*

PURPOSE: To set up a list of statement labels and/or switch designators which will be referred to by subsequent 'GO TO' statements.

FORM: 'SWITCH' $sw \leftarrow d_1, d_2, \ldots, d_n$

$sw:$ switch identifier
$d_1, d_2, \ldots, d_n:$ designational expression

RULES:

1. This statement defines the switch identifier *sw* as *being associated* with a list of designational expressions separated by commas.

2. A designational expression (d_i) is any one of the following:
   a. a statement label
   b. a switch designator. This has the form *sw[a]*, where *sw* represents a switch identifier and *a* represents an arithmetic expression.
   c. a conditional designator. This has the form

      'IF' b 'THEN' c 'ELSE' d

      where b represents a Boolean expression;
         c may be either a statement label, a switch designator or a conditional designator enclosed within parentheses;
         d may be either a statement label, a switch designator, or a conditional designator (not necessarily enclosed within parentheses).

3. Each designational expression is identified by a positive integer - the leftmost with 1, the next with 2, etc.

4. When a 'GO TO' statement involving a switch designator is encountered in the program, the subscript of the switch designator is given an integral value. It is this value which determines which element of the list is referenced.

5. If the list item referenced is a conditional designator the 'IF' clauses are evaluated until a designational expression involving only a label or a switch designator is reached.

6. If the list element referenced is a label, it specifies directly the next statement to be executed.

7. If the element is a switch designator, it in turn references another 'SWITCH' declaration. The subscript of the switch designator is evaluated to locate the correct list element of the new 'SWITCH' declaration.

8. This process may be repeated through any number of 'SWITCH' declarations until reference is made directly to a statement label.

9. Each time an element in the list of a 'SWITCH' declaration is referenced, any expressions the element may contain are re-evaluated.

EXAMPLE:

```
'SWITCH' BA←PA, 'IF' S 'THEN'
PB 'ELSE' PC, AC[X]
```

This switch may be called by a statement such as 'GO TO' BA[D] which operates as follows: If D has the value 1, operation is equivalent to operation of 'GO TO' PA, where PA is a statement label. If D has the value 2, operation is equivalent to operation of 'GO TO' 'IF' S 'THEN' PB 'ELSE' PC, where S is a Boolean expression and PB and PC are statement labels. If D has the value 3, operation is equivalent to operation of 'GO TO' AC[X] where AC is a switch identifier and X is an arithmetic expression. If D has any other value, the statement following the 'GO TO' is executed next.

Type Declarations

PURPOSE: *To specify which variables represent integer, real or Boolean quantities.*

FORM: type $v_1, v_2, \ldots, v_n$

type: *type word*
$v_1, v_2, \ldots, v_n$: *variable*

RULES:

1. *The type word may be one of the following:*
    a. 'REAL'
    b. 'INTEGER'
    c. 'BOOLEAN'

    The type word specifies the type of the variables $v_1, v_2, \ldots, v_n$.

2. *Each variable used in a program must be declared in a type declaration.*

3. *No variable may appear in more than one type declaration in a single block.*

4. *The type declaration is valid only for the block in which the declaration appears. Outside this block the identifiers may be used for other purposes.*

5. *The type declaration is valid for any blocks contained within the block containing the type declaration. However, variables may be redeclared in sub-blocks, in which case the previous declaration is superseded.*

Type

6. *When exit is made from a block (by* 'END' *or by a* 'GO TO'
*statement) all identifiers which were declared for the block
are undefined.*

EXAMPLE:
```
'BEGIN' 'INTEGER' P,Q; 'INTEGER' 'ARRAY' S[1:5];
        P←3; Q←2;
        'BEGIN' 'REAL' P,R;              These statements assign
                R←Q;                     the numbers 1,2,2,3,2, in
                P←1;                     this order to elements of
                S[1]←P;                  the array S.
                S[2]←Q;
                S[3]←R
        'END';
        S[4]←P;
        S[5]←Q
'END'
```

PURPOSE: *To specify which variables represent integer, real or Boolean quantities; to provide a means for retaining previous values of certain variables upon re-entry into a block.*

FORM: $\quad$ 'OWN' *type* $v_1, v_2, \ldots, v_n$

$$\begin{aligned} type: & \quad type\ word \\ v_1, v_2, \ldots, v_n: & \quad variable \end{aligned}$$

RULES:

1. *The type word may be one of the following:*
   a. 'REAL'
   b. 'INTEGER'
   c. 'BOOLEAN'

   The type word specifies the type of the variables $v_1, v_2, \ldots, v_n$.

2. *Each variable used in a program must appear in a type declaration.*

3. *No variable may appear in more than one type declaration in a single block.*

4. *Only variables whose values are to be preserved for possible re-entry into a block should be specified by an* 'OWN' *type declaration. All other variables should be declared in a regular type declaration.*

5. *The variable identifiers declared in any type declaration are defined only for the block in which they appear. Outside the block the identifiers may be used for other purposes.*

6. *When an exit is made from a block (by* 'END' *or by a* 'GO TO'
*statement) the identifiers are inaccessible although their
values have been saved.*

EXAMPLE:

```
        A←6;
    B:  'BEGIN' 'REAL' C; 'OWN' 'REAL' D;
                'IF' A 'EQ' 6 'THEN'
                'BEGIN'
                    C←7;
                    D←8;
                    A←9;
                    'GO TO' E
                'END';
                A←D-2
        'END';
    E:  'IF' A 'NQ' 6 'THEN' 'GO TO' B
```

*During the first execution
of block B, 7 is assigned to
C, 8 is assigned to D and 9
is assigned to A. Execution
of the conditional statement
labelled E causes block B
to be executed again. During
this execution, A is set to
6 because the previous value
of* 'OWN' *variable D is saved.
However, variable C could
not be used in this way
because not being* 'OWN', *its
value is not saved.*

V. Compound Statements and Blocks

PURPOSE: *To permit a series of statements to be joined together in such a way as to act as a unit.*

FORM: 'BEGIN' $s_1;s_2;\ldots;s_n$ 'END'

$s_1,s_2,\ldots,s_n$: *statement*

RULES:

1. *A compound statement may have a label and may contain any number of statements (s_i).*

2. *Each statement $s_1,s_2,\ldots,s_n$ may be*
   a. *a simple statement*
   b. *a compound statement*
   c. *a block*

3. *Each statement may have a label.*

4. *A 'GO TO' statement may transfer control to a statement within a compound statement.*

EXAMPLES:
1. I←1;   *These statements assign*
    T: 'IF' I 'LQ' 10 'THEN'   *the numbers one to ten to*
    'BEGIN'   *elements of the array A.*
      A[I]←I;   *This example contains a*
      I←I+1;   *compound statement as the*
      'GO TO' T   *true branch of a conditional*
    'END'   *statement.*

Compound statement

```
2.  'FOR' I←1 'STEP' 1 'UNTIL' 10 'DO'
        'BEGIN'
        'FOR' J←1 'STEP' 1 'UNTIL' 10 'DO'
            'BEGIN'
            'IF' I 'EQ' J 'THEN'
                    'BEGIN'
                    B[I,J]←1; 'GO TO' S
                    'END';
                B[I,J]←0;
          S: 'END'
        'END'
```

These statements generate a ten by ten unit matrix in the array B. Each 'FOR' statement has a compound statement as its object. Also, the true branch of the conditional statement is a compound statement.

PURPOSE: *To permit statements and declarations to be grouped together in such a way as to be independent of other parts of a program. This permits labels and identifiers to be used in different sections of a program without conflicts.*

FORM: $\text{'BEGIN'} \ d_1; d_2; \ldots; d_n; s_1; s_2; \ldots; s_m \ \text{'END'}$

$$d_1, d_2, \ldots, d_n: \quad declaration$$
$$s_1, s_2, \ldots, s_m: \quad statement$$

RULES:

1. *A block may have a label, and may contain any number of declarations and statements.*

2. *Each statement $s_1, s_2, \ldots, s_m$ may be*
   a. *a simple statement*
   b. *a compound statement*
   c. *a block*

3. *Each statement may have a label.*

4. *When a block is entered through* **'BEGIN'**, *the identifiers which are declared for the block are newly defined and lose any significance they may have had prior to entry.*

5. *All labels within a block are local to the block and may not be referred to from outside.*

6. When exit is made from a block, all identifiers which were declared for the block are undefined and may be used for other purposes, including those declared as 'OWN'.

7. If a declaration is prefaced with 'OWN', the identifiers so defined will retain their previous values upon re-entry into the block. If 'OWN' is not specified, the values will be lost when exit is made from the block and will be undefined upon re-entry.

8. All identifiers used in a program must be declared in one of the blocks comprising the program. No identifier may be declared more than once in a single block.

9. If blocks are nested, a statement label has meaning only in the smallest block containing that statement.

EXAMPLE:

```
'BEGIN' 'REAL' X,Y; 'ARRAY' A[1:5];
   X←1; Y←2;
   'BEGIN' 'REAL' X,Z;
           Z←Y;
           X←3;
           A[1]←X;
           A[2]←Y;
           A[3]←Z
   'END';
   A[4]←X;
   A[5]←Y
'END'
```

These statements assign the numbers 3,2,2,1,2 in this order to elements of the array A.

VI. *Input / Output*

INPUT/OUTPUT (I/O)

A. *Concepts*

   The ALGOL language which has been described in the previous sections of this book contains no provisions for effecting the input and output of data.

   Since I/O tends to be machine dependent, the authors of ALGOL 60 left to the individual implementors of the language the task of establishing their own conventions for input and output. Thus, a number of techniques for handling I/O exists.

   For example, additional statements and declarations may be added to the basic ALGOL language, i.e., 'READ', 'WRITE', 'FORMAT' etc.

   Another technique would be to have the compiler provide its own procedures which do the reading, writing, etc. To cause a desired I/O operation to be performed a user need only call the standard procedure, and specify the data and formatting details as procedure parameters.

   Part B of this section describes one computer manufacturer's method for providing I/O as part of the ALGOL language.

B. *Example of One Computer Manufacturer's ALGOL I/O Implementation*

The subject ALGOL compiler contains within it a number of procedures which handle the I/O. All a programmer need do is call the existing procedures using an ALGOL procedure statement, and through the procedure parameters, transmit the information required for the input and/or output process.

The procedure identifiers used by ALGOL are "reserved" and act as though declared in a block enclosing the program. If a programmer redeclares one of these identifiers in his program his declaration supersedes the standard definition. The procedures provided are listed below:

1. *Procedures pertaining to the layout of the I/O information on the external device:*

    BAD DATA

    FORMAT

    FORMAT n *(n=0,1,2,...,9)*

    HEND

    HLIM

    NO DATA

    TABULATION

    VEND

    VLIM

2. *Procedures dealing with the actual transmission of data:*

    INLIST

    INPUT n *(n=0,1,2,...,9)*

    OUTLIST

    OUTPUT n *(n=0,1,2,...,9)*

3. *Procedure allowing finer control over the input and output processes:*

    POSITION

    SYSPARAM

4. *Primitive procedures:*

    INSYMBOL
    LENGTH
    NAME
    OUTSYMBOL
    STRING ELEMENT
    TYPE

Each procedure is discussed in detail on the following pages, and the form of the procedure call is given.

In addition, the user of these procedures needs to provide a list of the data items which are to be transmitted. This list is specified in a user declared procedure called a list procedure. The identifier for this procedure is not reserved by ALGOL, and thus any valid identifier may be chosen. The list procedure is discussed following the ALGOL procedures.

1. Layout Procedures

The procedures to be described in this section deal with the
appearance of the data on an input or output device. All of the
procedures describe a printed page. However, the concepts may be
generalized to include any external device.

Listed below are the physical characteristics of the I/O devices.
The number of characters per line is referred to as P. The number
of lines per page is referred to as P'.

Device	P (characters)	P' (lines)
Line Printer	120	55
Card Reader (binary)	160	no limit
Card Reader (decimal)	80	no limit
Card Punch (binary)	160	no limit
Card Punch (decimal)	80	no limit
Magnetic Tape, Disk, Drum	120	no limit

These device characteristics may be changed where applicable (e.g.,
number of characters per line for magnetic tape may be changed) by
using the procedure SYSPARAM described in part 3 of this section.

The layout procedures are used to describe non-standard operations
which are to take place during input and output. The procedures
need not be called, in which case certain standard operations
(described with each procedure) will be in effect. The technique
for using the layout procedures is as follows:

Layout Procedures (cont'd)

The programmer declares a set-up procedure containing any or all
of the eight layout procedures (FORMAT, HLIM, VLIM, HEND, VEND,
NO DATA, TABULATION, BAD DATA). At some point in the program
there is a call to an I/O transmission procedure which has as one
of its parameters the procedure identifier of this set-up procedure.
At the time the I/O procedure is called it causes the set-up
procedure to be executed thus establishing the non-standard operations. Each time a new I/O transmission is called, the standard
layout operations will be resumed until changed by a new set-up
procedure.

PURPOSE: To indicate the procedure which is to be called when a request is made for an item to be transmitted, and the item is incompatible with the format character.

FORM: BAD DATA (p)

                                        p: procedure identifier

RULES:

1. This procedure applies only to input.

2. If a translated format (anything but I, E or L) is used and the referenced field is not compatible, control will be transferred to procedure p.

3. If BAD DATA is not used and the condition described in Rule 2 arises, control will be transferred to the end of the program as though a dummy label has been placed just before the final 'END'.

EXAMPLES:

1. BAD DATA (CHECK)   The procedure CHECK is used when incorrect data appears on the input device.

BAD DATA

```
2.  'BEGIN'
    'PROCEDURE' REDO; OUTLIST (6,LAY,LIST);
    ...
    BAD DATA (REDO);...
    'END'
```

When an incompatibility occurs, control goes to procedure REDO which outputs an error message.

PURPOSE: To describe the form in which data appears on the input device or is to appear on the output device.

FORM: FORMAT *(string)*

string: a string with a special form

RULES:

1. The format string is composed of a series of items separated by commas.

2. The string is interpreted from left to right in conjunction with a list of data items which are to be transmitted.

3. These data items usually appear in a separate procedure called a list procedure.

4. An item in the format string may describe a number, a string, or a Boolean quantity, or it may simply cause a title to be written or page alignment to take place.

5. The following rules describe the various kinds of format items.

6. *Number formats*
    a. Integers
        1) This format item consists of a series of Z's, a series of D's, or a series of Z's followed by D's each corresponding to a digit position of the number, and an optional sign.

2) *The letter* D *is used to indicate a digit which is always to be printed.*
   (ex. 385 when written with format DDDD *will appear externally as 0385.)*

3) *The letter* Z *is used to indicate that the corresponding digit is to be suppressed if it is a leading zero. In this case, a zero digit will be replaced by a blank space when all the digits to its left are zeros.*
   (ex. 21 when written with format ZZZ *will appear externally as* ƀ21.)

4) *A series of* Z's *or* D's *may be written in a shorthand notation as follows:* nZ *or* nD *(where n is an integer) is equivalent to* ZZZ...Z *or* DDD...D *(n times).*
   (ex. 3Z *and* ZZZ *are equivalent.* 4D *and* DDDD *are equivalent.)*

5) *An optional sign may precede or follow the* Z's *and* D's *of a number format.*
   If no sign appears, the number is assumed to be positive.
   Note: If a negative number is output with no sign position, the first digit position will print as ƀ,A,B, ...,I *representing the digits 0,1,2,...,9 respectively.*
   If a plus sign appears, the correct sign of the number appears on the external medium.
   If a minus sign appears, positive numbers will be unsigned and negative numbers will have a minus sign on the external medium.

6) If a preceding sign is to appear externally with a number which has had leading zeros suppressed, the sign will be placed immediately to the left of the first nonzero digit.

7) The total number of positions which an integer occupies on the external medium is the sum of the Z's and D's (plus one if the optional sign appears). If the field width is insufficient to hold the complete number, the high order digits are transmitted and the leftmost digit position will be ↑,J,K,...,R according as the acutal digit is 0,1,2,...,9. If, in addition to the above condition, the field is also unsigned and the number is negative, the leftmost position will be +,/,S,T,...,Z representing the digits is 0,1,2,...,9 respectively.

8) Examples of integer formats:
If +ZZDDD is used with 2176, it appears as ƀ+2176.
If -ZZZDD is used with 3, it appears as ƀƀƀƀ03.
If -DDDD is used with -45, it appears as -0045.
If ZZZ is used with 0, it appears as ƀƀƀ.
If ZZD is used with 0, it appears as ƀƀ0.
If 2Z4D+ is used with 390, it appears as ƀƀ0390+.

b. Decimal Numbers

1) This format item consists of Z's and/or D's each corresponding to a digit position, a period (.) or the letter V to indicate the position of the decimal point, and an optional sign.

2) *The letter* Z *has the same function it did for integers and it may appear only to the left of the decimal point.*

3) *The letter* D *may appear on both sides of the point and has the same function as for integers.*

4) *If a . is used to indicate the decimal point position, it will appear on the external medium in that position. If the letter* V *is used it merely indicates where the decimal point should be, but no space is used on the external medium.*

5) *The sign part functions as it did for integers.*

6) *The total number of positions which a decimal number occupies on the external medium is the sum of the* Z*'s and* D*'s plus one for the sign, plus one if the point is indicated by a . in the format. If the field width is insufficient to hold the complete number the high order digits are transmitted and the leftmost digit position will be* ↑,J,K,...,R *according as the actual digit is* 0,1,2,...,9. *If, in addition, the field is unsigned and the number is negative, the leftmost position will be* +,/,S,T, ...,Z *representing the digits* 0,1,2,...,9, *respectively.*

7) *Examples of decimal numbers:*

    If ZZDD.DD *is used with 146.776, it appears as* ƀ146.78.

    If -3D.D *is used with 1.2, it appears as* ƀ001.2.

    If +3Z.3D *is used with .0042, it appears as* ƀƀƀ+.004.

    If ZZDVD *is used with -142.78, it appears as* -1428.

    If ZZ4D.DD- *is used with -3394.7, it appears as*

        ƀƀ3394.70-.

    If ZZD *is used with 29.756, it appears as* ƀ30.

    If .3D- *is used with -.0254, it appears as* .025-.

c. *Decimal Numbers with Exponent*

1) *This format item is the same as that for a decimal number with the addition of an exponent part to indicate the power of ten to which the number must be raised to give the true decimal number.*

2) *The exponent part consists of an apostrophe (') to separate it from the decimal number followed by an optional sign, a series of* Z's *and/or a series of* D's.

3) *The* ' *will appear on the external medium in the proper position to separate the decimal number and its exponent.*

4) *The rules for the exponent part are the same as those for integers.*

5) *A number using this format will appear externally with its leading digit not zero. The exponent is adjusted accordingly. If the number is zero the exponent is also set to zero.*

6) If a nonzero number has a zero exponent which is specified by Z's the ' and the exponent sign are also suppressed.

7) The total number of positions needed on the external medium is the sum of all the Z's and D's plus one for the sign, plus one for the exponent sign, plus one for the ' plus one for the decimal point (if . is specified).

8) Examples of decimal numbers with exponents:

If 3D.DD'+DD is used with 3075.2, it appears as
307.52'+01.

If D.DD'-ZZ is used with 7.1, it appears as 7.10ƀƀƀƀ.

If ZZD'+ZD is used with .021758, it appears as
218'ƀ-4.

If DD'ZZ is used with 35.649, it appears as 36ƀƀƀ.

If .3D'+2D is used with 917.2, it appears as .917'+03.

If .DD'-ZZZ is used with .000312, it appears as
.31'ƀƀ-3.

d. Octal Numbers

1) The form of this item is nO or OO...O (n times) where n is an integer which specifies the number of digits in the octal field.

2) For output if n<12, the leftmost n digits will be transmitted; if n≥12, 12 digits will be transmitted followed by n-12 blanks.

3) For input if n<12, the next n characters are transmitted; if n≥12, the next 12 characters are transmitted.

4) *Examples of octal numbers:*

    If 50 *is used with* 447521767511 *on output, it appears*
        as 44752.

    If 140 *is used with* 712342165134 *on output, it appears*
        as 712342165134ƀƀ.

    If 150 *is used with* 754162314321744 *on input, it*
        appears as 754162314321 *internally.*

7. *Truncation for Number Formats*

   a. *The integer or decimal number formats described above may be followed by the letter* T *to indicate that the output should be truncated instead of rounded. Rounding occurs when truncation is not specified.*

   b. *Examples of truncation:*

    If -2Z3D.2DT *is used with* -12.719, *it appears as* ƀƀ-012.71.
    If 3ZDT+ *is used with* 145.6, *it appears as* ƀ145+.
    If -Z.DT'+ZZ *is used with* .012537, *it appears as* ƀ1.2'ƀ-2.

8. *Insertions in Number Formats*

   a. *All of the number formats may have either blanks or strings inserted anywhere within the format item. The insertion will appear on the external medium.*

   b. *A blank is denoted by the letter* B. *If more than one blank is desired it may be expressed by a series of* B's *or by the shorthand notation* nB *(n is an integer specifying the number of blanks.)* 3B *is equivalent to* BBB.

   c. *A string which is to be inserted must be enclosed in string quotes (i.e.,* "string\). *If the string is to be repeated it may appear as* n"string\ *where n is an integer specifying the number of times the string is to appear. The information in the string (not including the outermost quotes) is inserted in the corresponding place in the number.*

d. *Examples of insertions:*

    If D2B3D *is used with 3972, it appears as 3∅∅972.*

    If "ANS=\4D *is used with 271, it appears as ANS=0271.*

    If "INTEGER∅PART\-4ZVB"FRACTION\B2D *is used with -195.7634,*
          it appears as INTEGER∅PART∅-195∅FRACTION∅76.

    If 2ZB2D.DBT'+DD *is used with 44865.5, it appears as*
          44∅86.5∅'+01.

    If "OCTAL∅\5O *is used with 112233445566, it appears as*
          OCTAL∅11223.

9. *Numbers for Input*

a. *Numbers which are input using the above format codes should, in general, appear the same as those which are output.*

b. *However, there are fewer restrictions on the form of input numbers.*

    1) *Leading zeros may appear even if* Z's *are used in the format code. Leading blanks may appear even if* D's *are used.*

    2) *If insertion strings or blanks are used in the format code the corresponding number of characters on the input device are skipped.*

    3) *If a sign is specified at the left in the format code it may appear in any* Z *or* D *positions on the input device as long as it is to the left of the first digit. If the sign is specified at the right, it must appear exactly where it is indicated.*

10. *String Format*

   a. *This format item is used to output string quantities. It may not be used for input. Alpha format must be used instead.*

   b. *The form of this item is nS or SS...S (n times), where n is an integer which indicates the number of symbols in the string.*

   1) *If the actual string is longer than the number of S's indicated, only the leftmost symbols are transmitted.*

   2) *If the string is shorter, blank symbols are added to the right of the string.*

   3) *Examples of string format:*
   If S is used with "A\, it appears as A.
   If 6S is used with "TOTALS\, it appears as TOTALS.
   If SSS is used with "ABC\, it appears as ABC.
   If 4S is used with "PROGRAM\, it appears as PROG.
   If 5S is used with "CAT\, it appears as CAT∅∅.

11. *Insertions in String Format*

   a. *Blanks or strings may be inserted in the S format.*

   b. *The rules are the same as described for number formats.*

   c. *Examples:*
   If B3SBB2S is used with "12345\, it appears as ∅123∅∅45.
   If 2S"=\3SB is used with "T1ANS\, it appears as T1=ANS∅.

FORMAT

12. *Alpha Format*

    a. *This format item is used to transmit ALGOL basic symbols. (see INTRODUCTION for a list of basic symbols.)*

    b. 1) *The form of this item is the letter* A.

        2) *The appearance of the letter* A *as a format item causes transmission of a single symbol from or to the data item specified in the list procedure.*

        3) *The symbol will be stored as an integer.*

    c. *It may be desired to work with symbols transmitted by the* A *format. Therefore, a function is provided which makes any ALGOL symbol type* 'INTEGER' *and causes the symbol to have the same value as if it had been read in using Alpha format.*

    d. *The function is called* EQUIV. *Its argument must be an ALGOL basic symbol enclosed in string quotes, i.e.,* EQUIV("'BEGIN'\).

    e. *Example:*
        If A *format is used to read an* "*" *into variable ALG the statement* 'IF' ALG 'EQ' EQUIV ("*\) 'THEN' 'GO TO' GOOD *will check that* "*" *was in fact the symbol which was read in.*

13. *Boolean Format*

    a. *This format item is used to transmit Boolean quantities.*

    b. *The item may consist of the letter* P *or the letter* F.

c. If P *is used and the quantity is true, the number 1 is*
    transmitted; if false, 0 is transmitted.

d. If F *is used and the quantity is true the word* 'TRUE'
    transmitted; if false the word 'FALSE' *is transmitted.*

e. *Input must be in the form specified in c. and d.*

14. *Insertions in Boolean Format*

a. *Blanks or strings may be inserted in the Boolean format.*

b. *The rules are the same as described for number formats*
    and for strings.

c. *Examples:*
    If BBPB *is used with a Boolean variable whose value is*
    'TRUE'*, it appears as* ∅∅1∅*.*
    If "THE∅RELATION∅IS\BF *is used with a Boolean variable*
    whose value is 'FALSE'*, it appears as* THE∅RELATION∅IS∅'FALSE'*.*

15. *Standard Format*

a. *A number may be transmitted for input or output without*
    specifying in a format item the exact form the number is
    to take. The number appears on the I/O device in "standard
    format."

b. *If the letter* N *appears as a format item, it specifies*
    that a number with standard format is to be transmitted.

c. *Standard format for input may be defined as follows:*
    1) *Any number of digits in any of the forms which are*
        acceptable to integer or decimal number formats may
        be input.

FORMAT

      2) *The number must be terminated by an illegal character,*
      i.e., one not normally permitted in a number, or by
      k blanks where k is a system parameter initially set
      at one. k may be changed by calling the system proce-
      dure SYSPARAM *(described in Section C.).*

  d. *If standard format is invoked, and the first line referenced*
      contains any legal character for a number (i.e., digit,
      sign, decimal point or apostrophe) the right hand margin
      will terminate the number. If, however, the first line
      contains only nonlegal number characters, the subsequent
      lines will be searched until a legal number character is
      found. At this point the right hand margin is not significant,
      and only an illegal character or k blanks will terminate
      the number.

  e. *Standard format for output will appear as though the*
      decimal number format -.16D'+DD *had been invoked.*

  f. *Standard format will be assumed if the end of a format*
      string is reached while there are data items in the list
      procedure still to be transmitted. In this case all the
      remaining quantities will be transmitted with standard
      format.

  g. *If a list of variables is to be terminated but either*
      1) no reference is made to a FORMAT *procedure, or*
      2) the format call has the form FORMAT ("\)
      the items will be transmitted according to standard format.

16. *Untranslated Format*

    a. If a quantity is to be transmitted using the internal machine notation, a format item may consist simply of an I an R or an L.

    b. The letter to be used is determined as follows:
        I *for integers,*
        R *for real numbers,*
        L *for Boolean quantities.*

    c. Quantities which are written out using this format must be read in using the same format.

17. *Alignment Marks*

    a. These are single characters which cause specific page operations to occur.
        The operations are:
        / *go to next line*
        ↑ *go to new page*
        J *go to next tabulation position.*

    b. Alignment marks may appear as part of any format item. If they appear at the left of the item the actions take place before the format operation. If they appear at the right, they take place afterwards, i.e., /3S↑ causes a skip to a new line before the string is transmitted and a skip to a new page after.

FORMAT

    c.   *Alignment marks may also appear as separate format items simply by enclosing them in commas.*

    d.   *Any number of alignment marks may appear in succession, and this causes the specified action to be repeated as many times as it is indicated, i.e.,* ↑↑↑ *causes a page to be terminated and two pages to be skipped. Also any mark may be preceded by an integer n, where n indicates the number of times the action is to be done, i.e.,* 4⌡ *causes a skip to the fourth tab position and is equivalent to* ⌡⌡⌡⌡.

18.   <u>*Title Format*</u>

    a.   *This format item is used when it is desired to cause page alignment and/or the output of insertion strings without transmitting any ALGOL quantities.*

    b.   *This item consists entirely of insertions and alignment marks and refers to no data items.*

    c.   *On input this item causes characters to be skipped corresponding to the insertion strings and causes the desired alignment operations to be performed.*

    d.   *On output the insertion strings are transmitted and the alignment operations are performed.*

    e.   *Examples of title format:*
↑"SUMMARY\// *indicate a new page, an insertion, a line to be terminated and a line to be skipped.*
/"AMT\⌡"GROSS\⌡"NET\// *indicates a new line, an insertion, a tab, an insertion, a tab, an insertion, a line to be skipped.*

19. All the format items listed above constitute a format string.

20. Any format item or any group of format items can be repeated
     any number of times by enclosing in parentheses those items
     to be repeated and preceding the parentheses by an integer
     n indicating the number of repetitions desired, i.e., 3(2Z.D)
     causes 3 decimal numbers to be transmitted. If no integer
     precedes the parentheses an infinite number of repetitions
     is indicated.

EXAMPLES:

1. FORMAT("4D.2D,2Z,/P,   This format string transmits
    "ISØTHEØANS\↑,A\)   a decimal number and an
                                            integer on one line; on the
                                            next line is a Boolean quantity
                                            specified by a 0 or a 1
                                            followed by an insertion.
                                            Then a skip is made to a
                                            new page and an ALGOL symbol
                                            is transmitted.

2. FORMAT("7S,2(5Z.D'+ZZ,F),2J\)   A seven symbol string is
                                            transmitted followed by a
                                            decimal number, a Boolean
                                            quantity, a decimal number,
                                            a Boolean quantity. Then
                                            two tabulations occur.

3. FORMAT("(ZZ.BDT-,BBB+ZZD)\)   *A decimal number and an*
                                            integer are transmitted
                                            an indeterminate number
                                            of times, i.e., until the
                                            list of data items is ex-
                                            hausted.

PURPOSE: To describe the form in which data appears on the input
device or is to appear on the output device; to permit
certain elements of the format string to be variable and
to have their values calculated at the time the FORMAT
procedure is called.

FORM: FORMAT n (string, $x_1, x_2, \ldots, x_n$)

$n:$ integer

string: string with a
special form

$x_1, x_2, \ldots, x_n:$ expression

RULES:

1. n may be **0,1,2,...,9.** This value indicates the number of
    x's which appear following the format string.
    (Note: The form FORMAT (string) as discussed previously
    is simply a special case of this format call in which $n=0$.)

2. The form of the string is the same as that discussed for
    the procedure call FORMAT (string), with certain additional
    features.

3. The string may contain the letter X in various format items.
    The values of the x_i's which follow the format string will
    replace each X when the FORMAT procedure is called.

4. *The letter* X *may appear in the format string as follows:*

   a. *In a Number Format:*

   Any Z *or* D *may be preceded by the letter* X *to indicate a variable number of repetitions of the* Z *or* D.

   Examples:

   XZXD — *variable integer size*

   ZZ.XD — *variable number of decimal places*

   .DDD'XD — *variable exponent size*

   b. *In an Insertion:*

   The letter B *may be preceded by an* X *to indicate a variable number of blank spaces on output or a variable number of ignored positions on input.*

   Example:

   2ZXB3D.D

   c. *In a String Format:*

   The letter S *may be preceded by the letter* X *to indicate a variable number of symbols in the string.*

   Examples:

   XS

   BXSB4S

   d. *With an Alignment Mark:*

   ↑,/ *or* J *may be preceded by the letter* X *to indicate a variable number of times the specified alignment action is to be taken.*

   Examples:

   XJDD.DD — *variable number of tabulations*

   3S2BX/ — *variable number of lines to be skipped*

5. The X's may be used at most 9 times in a single format string. The integer *n* in the format call indicates the number of X's which appear in the string.

6. The $x_1, x_2, \ldots, x_n$ in the format call represent the integral values to be assigned to the X's in the string. $x_1, x_2, \ldots, x_n$ must be positive. x_1 is assigned to the first X which appears; x_2 to the second, etc.

EXAMPLE:

FORMAT 3 ("ZZXD.D,XBXS\,2,A-5,B)

The decimal number will be transmitted as though it had been written as ZZ2D.D. A-5 blanks will precede the string which will contain B symbols.

HEND

PURPOSE: *To specify the procedures which are to be called when the end of a line is reached during input or output; to permit special action to be taken depending on what situation causes the end-of-line condition to occur.*

FORM: HEND *(p1,p2,p3)*

p1,p2,p3: procedure identifier

RULES:

1. *p1 is the name of the procedure to be called when a "/" appears in the format call. This indicates that a new line is to begin and is considered the normal case.*

2. *p2 is the name of the procedure to be called when a group of characters is to be transmitted or a tabulation is specified which would pass the right margin of the current line as specified by* HLIM.

3. *p3 is the name of the procedure to be called when a group of characters is to be transmitted or a tabulation is specified which would pass the physical end of the line due to the characteristics of the I/O divice being used, but would not pass the right margin as set by* HLIM. *Note: This physical end is specified by standard limits set within the system or a control card to the system, and may be altered by procedure* SYSPARAM.

4. *If it is desired to take no special action when the end of a line is reached this procedure call may be omitted.*

5. *If action is desired for some but not all of the conditions, dummy procedure names may be used for those requiring no action.*

EXAMPLES:

1. HEND (NORM,OVER,END)

    a "/" in the format call causes control to go to Procedure NORM; if the right margin is reached control goes to OVER; if the physical end-of-line is reached control goes to END.

2. 'BEGIN'...'PROCEDURE' DUMMY;;...
    ...HEND (DUMMY,FIN,NEXT);...'END'

    Since Procedure DUMMY contains no statements, no special action will be taken when a "/" appears in the format call.

HLIM

PURPOSE: *To specify the left and right margins of the input or output lines.*

FORM: HLIM *(left, right)*

left, right: arithmetic expression

RULES:

1. *The first parameter specifies the left margin.*

2. *The second parameter specifies the right margin.*

3. *There is a restriction that 1 ≤ left ≤ right*

4. *If this procedure call is not given, the left margin is set to one and the right margin is set to infinity.*

EXAMPLES:

1. HLIM (5,50)   *Left margin is 5, right margin is 50.*

2. HLIM (J-4,K)   *Left margin is value of J-4, right is value of K.*

PURPOSE: *To indicate the procedure which is to be called when a request is made for data on an input device but no more data remains.*

FORM: NO DATA *(p)*

p: *procedure identifier*

RULES:

1. *This procedure call applies only to input.*

2. *If input data is requested by a data transmission procedure when no data remains on the input device, control will be transferred to procedure p.*

3. *If* NO DATA *is not used and the condition described in Rule 2 arises, control will be transferred to the end of the program as though a dummy label had been placed just before the final* 'END'.

EXAMPLES:
1. NO DATA (EOF)   *The procedure EOF is used when no data exists on the input device.*

NO DATA

2.   `'BEGIN'`
       `'PROCEDURE' LAST; 'GOTO' FIND;`
       `...`
       `NO DATA (LAST);...`
       `'END'`

When no data is found on the input device, control goes to procedure LAST which sends control to the statement labelled FIND.

PURPOSE: To set the width of the tabulation field of the I/O device; to permit the skipping of a fixed number of positions whenever the alignment mark J appears in a format call.

FORM: TABULATION (a)

                                        a: arithmetic expression

RULES:

1.   "a" specifies the number of characters of the foreign medium which constitute the tabulation field.

2.   If the left margin is at position X, the tab positions for a line are:
     X, X+a, X+2a, X+3a, ... , X+ka
     The last tab position occurs before or at the same point as the right margin as specified by HLIM, or at the physical end of the line, whichever is smaller.

3.   When a "J" appears in a format call, the I/O device is spaced to the next tab position.

4.   If this procedure call is not given the tabulation spacing is one.

TABULATION

EXAMPLES:

1. TABULATION (15)   *a new tab position occurs every 15 spaces.*

2. TABULATION (A↑2-B⁑C)   *The value of A^2-BC determines the tab spacing.*

166

PURPOSE: *To specify the procedures which are to be called when the end of a page is reached during input or output; to permit special action to be taken depending on what situation causes the end-of-page condition to occur.*

FORM: VEND *(p1,p2,p3)*

                                  p1,p2,p3: procedure identifier

RULES:

1. *p1 is the name of the procedure to be called when a "↑" appears in the format call. This indicates that the subsequent information is to appear on a new page, and is considered the normal case.*

2. *p2 is the name of the procedure to be called when a group of characters is to be transmitted which would appear on the line after the one specified by VLIM as the bottom margin.*

3. *p3 is the name of the procedure to be called when a group of characters is to be transmitted which would pass the physical end of the page due to the characteristics of the I/O device being used, but would not pass the bottom margin set by VLIM. Note: This physical end is specified by standard limits set within the system or a control card to the system, and may be altered by procedure SYSPARAM.*

4. *If it is desired to take no special action when the end of a page is reached this procedure call may be omitted.*

5. *If action is desired for some but not all of the conditions, dummy procedure names may be used for those requiring no action.*

EXAMPLES:

1. VEND (NEW,PAGE 1, PAGE 2)

   Control goes to procedure NEW when a "↑" appears in the format call; to PAGE 1 when the bottom margin is reached and to PAGE 2 when the physical end of the page is reached.

2. 'BEGIN'...'PROCEDURE' EMPTY;;...
   ...VEND (OK,FIX,EMPTY);...'END'

   No action is taken if an attempt is made to write beyond the end of the page.

PURPOSE: To set the vertical layout of a page; to specify how many
lines on a page are to be used.

FORM: VLIM *(top, bottom)*

                          top, bottom: arithmetic expression

RULES:

1. The top line of the page has a value of 1, the second,
    2, etc.

2. The first parameter indicates the first line to be used for
    transmission.

3. The second parameter indicates the last line to be used.

4. There is a restriction that $1 \leq top \leq bottom$.

5. If this procedure call is not given, the first line is set
    to one and the last line is set to infinity.

EXAMPLES:
    1. VLIM (10,50)   *Data transmission starts*
                                     on line 10 and ends on
                                     line 50.

2. VLIM (1, TOTAL)

Data transmission starts on the first line of a page, and ends on the line specified by the value of TOTAL.

Examples of Layout Procedures:

```
1.    'PROCEDURE' SET;
      'BEGIN'
        FORMAT ("3D.2D\);
        'IF' A 'EQ' B↑2 'THEN'
        'BEGIN'
            FORMAT ("ZZZ\);
            TABULATION (5)
        'END';
        VLIM ('IF' A 'EQ' B↑2 'THEN' 5
            'ELSE' 10,50)
      'END'
```

If $A=B^2$ the second format call will override the first, a TAB of 5 will be set and the vertical margins will be (5,50). If $A{\neq}B^2$ the first format will be in effect the TAB will be 1 and the vertical margins will be (10,50).

```
2.    'PROCEDURE' LAYOUT;
      'BEGIN'
        FORMAT ("↑,100(ZZD.D,BBD.D'DD),
            / \ );
        HLIM (5,60);
        HEND (GOOD,OVER,OVER)
      'END';
      'PROCEDURE' GOOD; HLIM (5,60);
      'PROCEDURE' OVER; HLIM (15,60)
```

Whenever line overflow occurs procedure OVER will change the horizontal margins. When the "/" in the format call is reached, procedure GOOD will restore the original margins.

2.   _Data Transmission Procedures_

_These procedures handle the actual transmission of data for input
and output._

_In calling these procedures it is necessary to specify the I/O
device which is to be used for the transmission. Files used by
ALGOL are restricted to the numeric file codes 01_{10} to 40_{10}.
05 is the standard input file and 06, the standard output file.
Error messages will thus be written on 06._

_The point in a program at which the actual I/O procedure is called
is when the transmission of data occurs. Layout procedures, if
any, and a list procedure, if any, will be called by the internal
I/O procedures._

PURPOSE: *To indicate that data is to be transmitted for input; to specify the input device, the set-up procedure and the list procedure.*

FORM: INLIST (a_1, a_2, a_3)

a_1: *arithmetic expression*
a_2, a_3: *procedure identifier*

RULES:

1. a_1 *is the file number which indicates the specific input device to be used.*

2. a_2 *is the name of the set-up procedure containing the layout procedure calls.*

3. a_3 *is the name of the list procedure which contains the data items to be transmitted.*

4. *When* **INLIST** *is executed, it first calls the layout procedures, then transfers back and forth to the list procedure while the actual input is taking place.*

EXAMPLES:

1. INLIST (05, ABC, INPT)   *This statement causes input to take place on I/O device 5 according to the layout procedures in procedure ABC and according to the list procedure INPT.*

INLIST

2. 'BEGIN' 'PROCEDURE' START;   *This program transmits a*
    'BEGIN'   *symbol into ALPHA, a real*
      FORMAT ("↑,A,D.D'DD/,ZDD,P\); *number into BOY, an integer*
      VLIM (2,50)   *into COUNT and a 0 or 1*
    'END';...   *into BOOL.*
    'PROCEDURE' LIST (OK);
    'BEGIN'
    OK (ALPHA); OK (BOY); OK (COUNT);
    OK (BOOL)
    'END';...
    INLIST (7,START,LIST);...
  'END'

PURPOSE: *To indicate that data is to be transmitted for input; to provide for data input without using layout procedures or a list procedure.*

FORM: INPUT *n* $(a, string, e_1, e_2, \ldots, e_n)$

n: *integer*

a: *arithmetic expression*

string: *format string*

$e_1, e_2, \ldots, e_n$: *variable or subscripted variable*

RULES:

1. *a is the file number which indicates the input device to be used.*

2. *The format string is in the same form as the format call* FORMAT *(string), i.e., no X's are allowed in the string.*

3. $e_1, e_2, \ldots, e_n$ *are the actual data items to be transmitted according to the format string given.*

4. *n may have the value* 0,1,2,...,9 *and indicates the number of data items.*

5. *The equivalent of this procedure call in terms of* INLIST *is as follows:*

```
'BEGIN' 'PROCEDURE' LAYOUT; FORMAT (string);
        'PROCEDURE' LIST (ITEM);
        'BEGIN' ITEM (e₁); ITEM (e₂);...;
                ITEM (eₙ)
        'END';
        INLIST (a,LAYOUT,LIST)
'END'
```

6. *When the only layout procedure required is* FORMAT *and when there are nine or fewer items to be transmitted, this simpler input call may be used instead of* INLIST.

EXAMPLES:

1. INPUT 6 (05, "(ZD.D)↑\,   *This transmits 6 values*
    A[1], A[2], A[3], A[4], A[5], A[6])*according to the repeated format ZD.D.*

2. INPUT 2 (07,"P,F\, B[1], B[2])   *This transmits 1 or 0 into* B_1 *and* 'TRUE' *or* 'FALSE' *into* B_2.

PURPOSE: *To indicate that data is to be transmitted for output; to specify the output device, the set-up procedure and the list procedure.*

FORM: OUTLIST (a_1, a_2, a_3)

a_1: *arithmetic expression*

a_2, a_3: *procedure identifier*

RULES:

1. a_1 *is the file number which indicates the specific output device to be used.*

2. a_2 *is the name of the set-up procedure containing the layout procedure calls.*

3. a_3 *is the name of the list procedure which contains the data items to be transmitted.*

4. *When* OUTLIST *is executed, it first calls the layout procedures then transfers back and forth to the list procedure while the actual output is taking place.*

OUTLIST

  1. OUTLIST (10,PAGE,LIST)   *This statement causes*
                    output to take place on
                    I/O device 10 according
                    to the layout procedures
                    in procedure PAGE and
                    according to the list
                    procedure LIST.

2. 'BEGIN' 'PROCEDURE' SET;   *This program causes the*
  FORMAT ("3D.D,BZZD,2B3S/\); *values of the two variables*
  ...   *TOTAL and INTEGER and the*
  'PROCEDURE' OUT (A);   *string ANS to be written*
  'BEGIN'   *out on device 6.*
   A (TOTAL); A (INTEGER); A ("ANS\)
  'END';...
  OUTLIST (6,SET,OUT);...
'END'

PURPOSE: *To indicate that data is to be transmitted for output; to provide for data output without using layout procedures or a list procedure.*

FORM: OUTPUT n $(a,string,e_1,e_2,\ldots,e_n)$

n: *integer*

a: *arithmetic expression*

string: *format string*

$e_1,e_2,\ldots,e_n$: *arithmetic expression, Boolean expression or string*

RULES:

1. *a is the file number which indicates the output device to be used.*

2. *The format string is in the same form as the format call* FORMAT *(string), i.e., no* X*'s are allowed in the string.*

3. *$e_1,e_2,\ldots,e_n$ are the actual data items to be transmitted according to the format string given.*

4. *n may have the value 0,1,...,9 and indicates the number of data items.*

5. *The equivalent of this procedure call in terms of* OUTLIST
    is as follows:

```
'BEGIN' 'PROCEDURE' LAYOUT; FORMAT (string);
        'PROCEDURE' LIST (ITEM);
        'BEGIN' ITEM (e₁); ITEM (e₂);...;
                ITEM (eₙ)
        'END';
        OUTLIST   (a,LAYOUT,LIST)
'END'
```

6. *When the only layout procedure required is* FORMAT *and when
    there are nine or fewer items to be transmitted, this
    simpler output call may be used instead of* OUTLIST.

EXAMPLES:

1. OUTPUT 3 (06,"3(2ZD.DD)\,A,B,C)   *This statement will cause
    3 values of A, B and C to
    be transmitted to device
    6 according to the format
    given.*

2. OUTPUT 5 (09,"2(D.D'ZZ), 3S,   *This statement will cause
    2BSS,I\, X↑2-3,Y↑2-3,"TOT\,   2 decimal numbers, 2 strings
    "A1\, COUNT)   and an internal notation
    integer to be transmitted.*

3.   _Input/Output Control Procedures_

These procedures access system parameters and allow some control
over the positioning of the I/O devices.

PURPOSE: To position the specified file to the indicated page and line.

FORM: POSITION (e_1, e_2, e_3)

e_1, e_2, e_3: arithmetic expression

RULES:

1. e_1 represents the file number specifying the I/O device concerned.

2. e_2 is the page number.

3. e_3 is the line number.

4. This procedure may be used in conjunction with SYSPARAM to record information on a file and later make reference to it. At a particular point in a program, a call on SYSPARAM can be used to record the current position on a file. At a later time, if it is desired to return to that point in the file a call on POSITION giving the relevant page and line numbers for parameters e_2 and e_3 will reposition the file to the desired point. Note: Backpositioning on a unit record device is undefined; however, such positioning is meaningful for a unit record logical device which is assigned to a magnetic tape (other than SYSOUT).

EXAMPLE:

POSITION (4,A-5,B)   Device 4 will be spaced so that it is prepared to access the line specified by the value of B on the page specified by the value of A-5.

SYSPARAM

PURPOSE: To gain access to certain system parameters so that they may be modified.

FORM: SYSPARAM (a_1, a_2, a_3)

a_1, a_2: arithmetic expression
a_3: integer variable

RULES:

1. The system parameters which may be changed or read out are:
    a. The character, line and page pointers $(p, p'$ and $p'')$ respectively.
    b. The "standard format" constant determining the number of spaces between items (k).
    c. The physical end of line (P) and the physical end of page (P') which are characteristic of the I/O device.

2. a_1 is the file number specifying the I/O device concerned.

3. a_2 may have a value of $1, 2, \ldots, 11$.
    a. If the value of a_2 is $1, 3, 5, 7, 9$ or 11, the value of the system parameter in question is assigned to variable a_3.
    b. If the value of a_2 is $2, 4, 6, 8$ or 10, the value of a_3 becomes the new value of the system parameter.

c. *The action is as follows:*

if $a_2 = 1$, $a_3 \leftarrow p$	*if $a_2 = 2$, $p \leftarrow a_3$*
if $a_2 = 3$, $a_3 \leftarrow p'$	*if $a_2 = 4$, $p' \leftarrow a_3$*
if $a_2 = 5$, $a_3 \leftarrow P$	*if $a_2 = 6$, $P \leftarrow a_3$*
if $a_2 = 7$, $a_3 \leftarrow P'$	*if $a_2 = 8$, $P' \leftarrow a_3$*
if $a_2 = 9$, $a_3 \leftarrow k$	*if $a_2 = 10$, $k \leftarrow a_3$*
if $a_2 = 11$, $a_3 \leftarrow p''$	

4. *p and p' represent actual positions on the I/O device which are to be changed when $a_2 = 2$ and $a_2 = 4$.*

   a. *If $a_2 = 2$, p is tested to see if $p < a_3$. If it is, blanks are inserted until $p = a_3$. If $p \geq a_3$, a skip to the next line is performed, p is set equal to 0, and blanks are inserted until $p = a_3$.*

   b. *If $a_2 = 4$, p' is tested to see if $p' < a_3$. If it is, lines are advanced until $p' = a_3$. If $p' \geq a_3$, a skip is made to a new page, p' is set equal to 0, and lines are advanced until $p' = a_3$.*

5. *$a_2 = 6$ and $a_2 = 8$ change the physical limits of the I/O device (P and P') where this is possible (i.e., magnetic tape block length may be changed and unit record devices may have physical limits reduced, but not extended beyond the standard limits). If the limits cannot be changed and these actions are specified, the statement acts like a dummy statement.*

SYSPARAM

6. a_2 may also have a value of 21 or 22
   a. If the value of a_2 is 21, the file denoted by a_1 is defined as an input file.
   b. If the value of a_2 is 22, the file denoted by a_1 is defined as an output file.
   c. If the value of a_2 is 21 or 22, the value of a_3 is not significant.

7. The condition which requires a_2 = 21 or 22 only arises when the intended first action on a particular file uses a primitive procedure or procedure SYSPARAM. If this is the case, the system does not know the nature of the file and thus a call to SYSPARAM with a_2 = 21 or 22 would serve to define the file. e.g., If the first action with respect to file 6 is to read out the value of p by a call to SYSPARAM such as

   SYSPARAM (06,1,CHAR)

   this call would have to be preceded by a call to SYSPARAM defining 06 as an output file as follows:

   SYSPARAM (06,22,0)

EXAMPLES:

1. SYSPARAM (8,3,LINENO)   On device 8 the value of the line pointer is assigned to variable LINENO.

2. SYSPARAM (5,10,3)   For device 5 the value of k is changed to 3, i.e., 3 or more blanks must follow a number in standard format.

4. *Primitive Procedures*

    These procedures are included in the ALGOL language to allow the
    other Input/Output procedures to be written in ALGOL.

    They are available for use by the programmer but are not intended
    to be general purpose routines.

PURPOSE: *To associate specific ALGOL symbols with specific integers; to read in a basic symbol from an external device as an integer.*

FORM: INSYMBOL (e, s, v)

e: *arithmetic expression (called by value)*
s: *string*
v: *integer variable*

RULES:

1. *The basic symbols contained in the string "s" are given integer values.*

2. *The symbols are assigned from left to right to the positive integers 1,2,3, etc.*

3. *This procedure acts as follows:*
   a. *It reads in the next symbol from the input device.*
   b. *If it is a basic symbol which appears in the string "s", the variable v will be assigned the integer value associated with this symbol.*
   c. *If it is a basic symbol which does not appear in the string "s", v will receive a value of 0.*
   d. *If the input symbol is not an ALGOL basic symbol, v will receive a value of minus one.*

e. *If there is no more data on the input device, v will receive a value of minus two.*

f. *If the string "s" is null, i.e., INSYMBOL (e,"\,v), v will receive the standard system value for the basic symbol.*

PURPOSE: *To calculate the length of a given string.*

FORM: LENGTH *(s)*

RULES:

    1.   *The result of this procedure is an integer.*

    2.   *It is equal to the number of basic symbols in the string "s" not including the outermost pair of string quotes.*

NAME

PURPOSE: *To permit the saving or "remembering" of labels and procedure identifiers.*

FORM: NAME (v_1, v_2, a, p)

v_1, v_2: *integer variable*
a: *statement label*
p: *procedure identifier*

RULES:

1. *If v_1 has a value of 1, the integer associated with a is assigned to v_2.*

2. *If v_1 has a value of 3, the integer associated with p is assigned to v_2.*

3. *If v_1 has a value of 2, control will be transferred to the label whose value is the same as that of v_2.*
   (Note: v_2 must have been assigned the value of a label by a previous NAME statement.)
   If $v_2 = 0$ the program will be terminated.

4. *If v_1 has a value of 4, control will be transferred to the procedure whose identifier has the same value as v_2.*
   (Note: v_2 must have been assigned the value of a procedure identifier by a previous NAME statement.)
   If $v_2 = 0$ the procedure will be a dummy procedure.

5. *The association of specific integers with labels and procedure identifiers holds only in the block in which the labels or identifiers are declared, i.e., the rules of scope for ALGOL block structure are obeyed.*

OUTSYMBOL

PURPOSE: *To associate ALGOL basic symbols with specific integers;*
            to write out a basic symbol on an external device from
            an internally stored integer.

FORM: OUTSYMBOL (e_1, s, e_2)

                                        e_1, e_2:   *arithmetic expression*
                                                  (called by value)
                                             s: *string*

RULES:

1. *The basic symbols in the string "s" are given integer values.*

2. *The positive integers 1,2,3, etc. are assigned to the symbols from left to right; leftmost = 1, next = 2, etc.*

3. *This procedure acts as follows:*
   a. *It evaluates e_2 and determines the integer which is closest to this value.*
   b. *If the value has an equivalent in string "s", the basic symbol corresponding to this value will be written on the output device.*
   c. *If the value has no equivalent in string "s" by being outside the bounds of the string, or if it is not a basic symbol, the symbol ⌀ will be written on the output device.*
   d. *If the string "s" is null, i.e., OUTSYMBOL $(e_1, "\backslash, e_2)$, the standard system values are used to determine the basic symbol which will be written on the output device.*

PURPOSE: *To enable the scanning of a given string (actual or formal) in a machine independent manner.*

FORM: STRING ELEMENT (s_1, v_1, s_2, v_2)

s_1, s_2: *string*
v_1, v_2: *variable*

RULES:

1. *Variable v_1 determines which symbol of s_1 is referenced, i.e., if $v_1 = 1$ it is the leftmost symbol; if $v_1 = 2$, the next, etc.*

2. *Once the symbol is chosen, its associated integer is assigned to variable v_2.*
   (Note: the associated integer is determined by encoding string s_2 as was done with the string in the procedure INSYMBOL.)

TYPE

PURPOSE: *To determine the type of a number which is to be written out in standard format.*

FORM: TYPE (v_1, v_2)

v_1:   *variable*

v_2:   *variable or string*

RULES:

1. *If v_2 is a string, v_1 is set equal to 4.*

2. *If v_2 is a variable, v_1 is assigned a different value depending on the type of v_2 as follows:*
   a. *If v_2 is* 'INTEGER', $v_1 \leftarrow 1$.
   b. *If v_2 is* 'REAL', $v_1 \leftarrow 2$.
   c. *If v_2 is* 'BOOLEAN', $v_1 \leftarrow 3$.

5. _List Procedure_

   _This procedure is written by the programmer to be used with the
   I/O procedures provided by ALGOL._

PURPOSE: *To list a sequence of quantities to be transmitted for input or output; this list is used in conjunction with the format items of a FORMAT call.*

FORM: 'PROCEDURE' *name (ident); s*

> name: *procedure identifier*
> ident: *identifier*
> s: *simple statement,*
>   *compound statement or*
>   *block*

RULES:

1. *The formal parameter "ident" appears in the body of the list procedure as a procedure identifier.*

2. *Each item to be transmitted for input or output appears in the procedure body as the parameter for procedure ident.*
   Example:
   > 'PROCEDURE' A (X); 'BEGIN' X (M); X (N); X (P) 'END'
   M, N and P are transmitted.

3. *When the list procedure is called by a data transmission procedure (INLIST or OUTLIST), an internal system procedure (INITEM or OUTITEM) will be the actual parameter corresponding to the formal parameter "ident," and thus will be substituted for "ident" in the list procedure body.*

4. *Execution of the list procedure causes the internal system procedure (*INITEM *or* OUTITEM*) to be executed.* INITEM *or* OUTITEM *has as its parameter the item to be transmitted.*

5. *This parameter may be an arithmetic expression, Boolean expression or a string for output. However, the parameter may be only a variable or subscripted variable for input.*

6. *The item is called by name by the internal system procedure and its value is transmitted for input or output.*

7. *The sequence of statements in the list procedure body determines the sequence in which the items are transmitted for input or output.*

8. *All ALGOL statements are permissible in a list procedure including a call to one or more of the layout procedures.*

EXAMPLES:

1.
```
'PROCEDURE' LIST (NAME);
'BEGIN' NAME (X); NAME (Y↑3*Z);
NAME ("TOTAL\) 'END'
```
   The identifier NAME is replaced by a system procedure name when the list procedure is called. $X, Y\uparrow3*Z$ *and* "TOTAL\ *are parameters to this system procedure and their values will be transmitted.*

2.
```
'PROCEDURE' MANY (ITEM);
'FOR' I←1 'STEP' 1 'UNTIL'
10 'DO' 'BEGIN' ITEM (A[I]);
ITEM (B[I]) 'END'
```
   The items to be transmitted are $A_1, B_1, A_2, B_2, \ldots, A_{10}, B_{10}$.

VII. *Appendices*

Appendix 1
Reserved Identifiers

RESERVED IDENTIFIERS

The following list enumerates reserved identifiers. These identify functions provided by the compiler and, in the case of our Input Output technique, the internal I/O procedures. These functions and procedures which are available without explicit declarations, are assumed to be declared in a block external to the program. However, a programmer may redeclare a reserved identifier, in which case the reserved meaning is superseded.

NOTE: Since the ALGOL words as described in the Introduction were enclosed in apostrophes they are not reserved words and may be used freely as identifiers. In certain compilers, however, they are reserved, and may be used only in the context provided by their definition.

The reserved identifiers are as follows:

1. Functions:

ABS	EXP
ARCTAN	LN
COS	SIGN
ENTIER	SIN
EQUIV	SQRT

2. I/O procedures:

BAD DATA	FORMAT 5
FORMAT	FORMAT 6
FORMAT 0	FORMAT 7
FORMAT 1	FORMAT 8
FORMAT 2	FORMAT 9
FORMAT 3	HEND
FORMAT 4	HLIM

2. *I/O procedures: (cont'd)*

INLIST	OUTPUT 1
INPUT 0	OUTPUT 2
INPUT 1	OUTPUT 3
INPUT 2	OUTPUT 4
INPUT 3	OUTPUT 5
INPUT 4	OUTPUT 6
INPUT 5	OUTPUT 7
INPUT 6	OUTPUT 8
INPUT 7	OUTPUT 9
INPUT 8	OUTSYMBOL
INPUT 9	POSITION
INSYMBOL	STRINGELEMENT
LENGTH	SYSPARAM
NAME	TABULATION
NODATA	TYPE
OUTLIST	VEND
OUTPUT 0	VLIM

Appendix 2
Mathematical Functions

Form	Description
ABS(e)	absolute value of the expression e
ARCTAN(e)	principal value of the arctangent of e
COS(e)	cosine of e
ENTIER(e)	the integral part of e
EXP(e)	exponential function of e
LN(e)	natural logarithm of e
SIGN(e)	sign of e (+1 if e>0, 0 if e = 0, -1 if e<0)
SIN(e)	sign of e
SQRT(e)	square root of e

These functions are available without explicit declarations. They are assumed to be declared in a block external to the program. However, a programmer may redeclare a mathematical function identifier, in which case the standard meaning is superseded.

These functions accept parameters of types 'REAL' and 'INTEGER'. They all yield values of type 'REAL', except for ENTIER(e) and SIGN(e) which yield values of type 'INTEGER'.

The parameters of these functions are treated as 'VALUE' parameters.

Appendix 3
A Set of Representative
Algol Programs

The following Algorithms have appeared in the "Communications of the ACM" journals. They have been included in this book so that the reader may solidify his knowledge of the ALGOL language by seeing some actual programs which have been written for various existing ALGOL compilers.

The specific ACM journal in which the program appeared and the author's name have been included for each program. The only change which has been made is in the form of presentation of the example. In the ACM journals the algorithms are written in ALGOL reference language as opposed to a specific hardware representation of ALGOL. Since, throughout this book, ALGOL has been described using the acceptable symbols of an actual ALGOL compiler, the journal algorithms have been transcribed to conform to the list of basic symbols as given in the Introduction of this text.

Example: #1

Name: EVALUATION OF DETERMINANT

Origin: Communications of the ACM, April 1964, P 243, Algorithm 224

Author: Leo J. Rotenberg, Box 2400, 362 Memorial Dr., Cambridge, Mass.

Problem

```
'REAL' 'PROCEDURE' DETERMINANT (A,N);
   'VALUE' N;  'REAL' 'ARRAY' A;  'INTEGER' N;
'COMMENT' THIS PROCEDURE EVALUATES A DETERMINANT BY TRIANGULARI-
   ZATION.  THE MATRIX SUPPLIED BY THE CALLING PROCEDURE IS MODIFIED
   BY THIS PROGRAM.  THIS PROCEDURE IS AN EXTENSIVE REVISION AND
   CORRECTION OF ALGORITHM 41;
'BEGIN' 'REAL' PRODUCT,FACTOR,TEMP,DIV,PIV,ABPIV, MAXPIV;
   'INTEGER' SSIGN,I,J,R,IMAX;
   SSIGN ← 1;  PRODUCT ← 1.0;
   'FOR' R ← 1 'STEP' 1 'UNTIL' N-1 'DO'
   'BEGIN' MAXPIV ← 0.0;
      'FOR' I ← R 'STEP' 1 'UNTIL' N 'DO'
      'BEGIN' PIV ← A[I,R];
         ABPIV ← ABS(PIV);
         'IF' ABPIV 'GR' MAXPIV 'THEN'
         'BEGIN' MAXPIV ← ABPIV;
            DIV ← PIV;
            IMAX ← I
         'END'
      'END';
      'IF' MAXPIV 'NQ' 0.0 'THEN'
      'BEGIN' 'IF' IMAX 'EQ' R 'THEN' 'GOTO' RESUME 'ELSE'
         'BEGIN' 'FOR' J ← R 'STEP' 1 'UNTIL' N 'DO'
            'BEGIN' TEMP ← A[IMAX,J];
               A[IMAX,J] ← A[R,J];
```

```
                A[R,J] ← TEMP
          'END';
          SSIGN ← - SSIGN;
          'GOTO' RESUME
       'END'
    'END';
    DETERMINANT ← 0.0
    'GOTO' RETURN;
RESUME: 'FOR' I ← R+1 'STEP' 1 'UNTIL' N 'DO'
    'BEGIN' FACTOR ← A[I,R]/DIV;
       'FOR' J ← R+1 'STEP' 1 'UNTIL' N 'DO'
       A[I,J] ← A[I,J] - FACTOR ⋇ A[R,J]
    'END'
'END';
'FOR' I ← 1 'STEP' 1 'UNTIL' N 'DO'
PRODUCT ← PRODUCT ⋇ A[I,I];
'COMMENT' EXPONENT OVERFLOW OR UNDERFLOW WILL MOST LIKELY
    OCCUR HERE IF AT ALL.  FOR LARGE OR SMALL DETERMINANTS THE USER
    IS CAUTIONED TO REPLACE THIS WITH A CALL TO A MACHINE-LANGUAGE
    PRODUCT ROUTINE WHICH WILL HANDLE EXTREMELY LARGE OR SMALL
    REAL NUMBERS;
DETERMINANT ← SSIGN ⋇ PRODUCT;
RETURN:
'END'
```

Notes:

This program has been included to illustrate the following:

1. a procedure declaration in the form of a block

2. compound statements as objects of 'FOR' *statements.*

Example: #2

Name: LOGARITHM OF A COMPLEX NUMBER

Origin: Communications of the ACM, November 1964, P 660, Algorithm 243

Author: David S. Collens, Computer Laboratory, The University,
Liverpool 3, England

Problem

```
'PROCEDURE' LOGC (A, B, C, D, FAIL); 'VALUE' A, B, FAIL; 'REAL'
   A, B, C, D; 'LABEL' FAIL;
'COMMENT' THIS PROCEDURE COMPUTES THE NUMBER C + DI WHICH IS
   EQUAL TO THE PRINCIPAL VALUE OF THE NATURAL LOGARITHM OF A + BI,
   I.E., SUCH THAT -PI 'LS' D 'LQ' +PI.  A NONLOCAL LABEL MUST BE SUPPLIED
   AS A PARAMETER OF THE PROCEDURE, TO BE USED AS AN EXIT WHEN THE
   REAL PART OF THE RESULT BECOMES -INFINITY.  WHERE REQUIRED IN THE BODY
   OF THE PROCEDURE THE NUMERICAL VALUES FOR PI, PI/2, AND THE LOG-
   ARITHM OF THE SQUARE ROOT OF 8 ARE PROVIDED;
   'IF' A 'EQ' 0 'OR' B 'EQ' 0 'THEN' 'GOTO' FAIL
   'ELSE'
   'BEGIN'
       'REAL' E,F;
       E ← 0.5 × A; F ← 0.5 × B;
       'IF' ABS(E) 'LS' 0.5 'OR' ABS(F) 'LS' 0.5 'THEN'
       'BEGIN'
          C ← ABS(2×A) + ABS(2×B);
          D ← 8 × A/C × A + 8 × B/C × B;
          C ← 0.5 × (LN(C)+LN(D))-1.03972077084
       'END'
       'ELSE'
       'BEGIN'
          C ← ABS(0.5×E) + ABS(0.5×F);
```

Example: #2 *(cont'd)*

```
       D ← 0.5 ⋇ E/C ⋇ E + 0.5 ⋇ F/C ⋇ F;
       C ← 0.5 ⋇ (LN(C)+LN(D)) + 1.03972077084
   'END';
   D ← 'IF' A 'NQ' 0 'OR' ABS(E) 'GQ' ABS(F) 'THEN' ARCTAN(B/A) +
      ('IF' SIGN(A) 'NQ' -1'THEN' 0 'ELSE' 'IF' SIGN(B) 'NQ' -1'THEN'
          3.14159265359 'ELSE' -3.14159265359) 'ELSE' - ARCTAN(A/B)
          + 1.57079632679 ⋇ SIGN(B)
'END' LOGC
```

<u>*NOTES:*</u>

This program has been included to illustrate the following:

1. *compound statements as objects of conditional statements*
2. *the use of mathematical functions in arithmetic expressions*
3. *nested 'IF' clauses in an arithmetic expression.*

Problem


```
'PROCEDURE' MATRIXPERM(A,B,J,K,S,D,N,P);  'VALUE' N; 'REAL' A,B;
   'INTEGER''ARRAY' S,D; 'INTEGER' J,K,N,P;
'COMMENT' A PROCEDURE USING JENSEN'S DEVICE WHICH EXCHANGES
   ROWS OR COLUMNS OF A MATRIX TO ACHIEVE A REARRANGEMENT SPECIFIED
   BY THE PERMUTATION VECTORS S,D[1:N].  ELEMENTS OF S SPECIFY THE
   ORIGINAL SOURCE LOCATIONS WHILE ELEMENTS OF D SPECIFY THE DESIRED
   DESTINATION LOCATIONS.  NORMALLY A AND B WILL BE CALLED AS SUB-
   SCRIPTED VARIABLES OF THE SAME ARRAY.  THE PARAMETERS J,K NOM-
   INATE THE SUBSCRIPTS OF THE DIMENSION AFFECTED BY THE PERMUTA-
   TION, P IS THE JENSEN PARAMETER.  AS AN EXAMPLE OF THE USE OF THIS
   PROCEDURE, SUPPOSE R,C[1:N] TO CONTAIN THE ROW AND COLUMN SUB-
   SCRIPTS OF THE SUCCESSIVE MATRIX PIVOTS USED IN A MATRIX INVER-
   SION OF AN ARRAY A[1:N,1:N];  I.E., R[1], C[1] ARE THE RELATIVE SUB-
   SCRIPTS OF THE FIRST PIVOT R[2], C[2] THOSE OF THE SECOND PIVOT AND
   SO ON.  THE TWO CALLS
            MATRIXPERM (A[J,P],A[K,P],J,K,R,C,N,P)
            AND MATRIXPERM (A[P,J],A[P,K],J,K,C,R,N,P)
   WILL PERFORM THE REQUIRED REARRANGEMENT OF ROWS AND COLUMNS
      RESPECTIVELY;
'BEGIN' 'INTEGER' 'ARRAY' TAB,LOC[1:N]; 'INTEGER'I,T; 'REAL'W;
'COMMENT' SET UP INITIAL VECTOR TAG NUMBER AND ADDRESS ARRAYS;
   'FOR' I ← 1 'STEP' 1 'UNTIL' N 'DO' TAG[I] ← LOC[I] ← I;
'COMMENT' START PERMUTATION;
   'FOR' I ← 1 'STEP' 1 'UNTIL' N 'DO'
```

Example: #3 (cont'd)

```
'BEGIN' T ← S[I]; J ← LOC[T]; K ← D[I];
    'IF' J 'NQ' K 'THEN' 'BEGIN' 'FOR' P ← 1'STEP' 1'UNTIL' N 'DO'
                        'BEGIN' W ← A; A ← B; B ← W 'END';
                        TAG[J] ← TAG[K]; TAG[K] ← T;
                        LOC[T] ← LOC[TAG[J]]; LOC[TAG[J]] ← J
                'END' JK CONDITIONAL
    'END' I LOOP
'END' MATRIXPERM
```

NOTES:

This program has been included to illustrate the following:

1. nested compound statements

2. subscripts which are themselves subscripted variables

3. comments after 'END'.

Example: #4

Name: MATRIX INVERSION

Origin: Communications of the ACM, June 1964, P 347, Algorithm 231

Author: J. Boothroyd, Electric-Leo Computers, Kidsgrove, Stoke-on-Trent, England

Problem

```
'PROCEDURE'  MATRIXINVERT (A,N,EPS,SINGULAR); 'VALUE' N,EPS;'AR
    RAY'A; 'INTEGER' N; 'REAL' EPS; 'LABEL' SINGULAR;
'COMMENT' INVERTS A MATRIX IN ITS OWN SPACE USING THE GAUSS-
    JORDAN METHOD WITH COMPLETE MATRIX PIVOTING.  I.E., AT EACH
    STAGE THE PIVOT HAS THE LARGEST ABSOLUTE VALUE OF ANY ELEMENT IN
    THE REMAINING MATRIX.  THE COORDINATES OF THE SUCCESSIVE MATRIX
    PIVOTS USED AT EACH STAGE OF THE REDUCTION ARE RECORDED IN THE
    SUCCESSIVE ELEMENT POSITIONS OF THE ROW AND COLUMN INDEX
    VECTORS R ANC C.  THESE ARE LATER CALLED UPON BY THE PROCEDURE
    MATRIXPERM WHICH REARRANGES THE ROWS AND COLUMNS OF THE
    MATRIX.  IF THE MATRIX IS SINGULAR THE PROCEDURE EXITS TO AN APPRO-
    PRIATE LABEL IN THE MAIN PROGRAM;
'BEGIN' 'INTEGER' I,J,K,L,PIVI,PIVJ,P; 'REAL' PIVOT; 'INTEGER' 'ARRAY'
    R,C[1:N];
'COMMENT' SET ROW AND COLUMN INDEX VECTORS;
    'FOR' I ← 1'STEP' 1'UNTIL' N 'DO' R[I] ← C[I] ← I;
'COMMENT' FIND INITIAL PIVOT; PIVI ← PIVJ ← 1;
    'FOR' I ← 1'STEP' 1'UNTIL' N 'DO' 'FOR' J ← 1'STEP' 1'UNTIL' N 'DO'
        'IF' ABS (A[I,J]) 'GR' ABS (A[PIVI,PIVJ]) 'THEN' 'BEGIN' PIVI ← I;
        PIVJ ← J 'END';
'COMMENT' START REDUCTION;
    'FOR' I ← 1'STEP' 1'UNTIL' N 'DO'
    'BEGIN' L ← R[I]; R[I] ← R[PIVI]; R[PIVI] ← L; L ← C[I];
```

Example: #4 (cont'd)

```
    C[I] ← C[PIVJ]; C[PIVJ] ← L;
    'IF' EPS 'GR' ABS(A[R[I],C[I]]) 'THEN'
    'BEGIN' 'COMMENT' HERE INCLUDE AN APPROPRIATE OUTPUT PRO-
        CEDURE TO RECORD I AND THE CURRENT VALUES OF R[1:N] AND
        C[1:N]; 'GOTO' SINGULAR 'END';
  'FOR' J ← N 'STEP' -1'UNTIL'I+1,I-1'STEP'-1'UNTIL' 1'DO' A[R[I],C[J]]
    ← A[R[I],C[J]]/A[R[I],C[I]]; A[R[I],C[I]] ← 1/A[R[I],C[I]];
    PIVOT ← 0;
  'FOR' K ← 1'STEP' 1'UNTIL' I-1, I+1'STEP' 1'UNTIL' N 'DO'
      'BEGIN' 'FOR' J ← N'STEP' -1'UNTIL' I+1,I-1'STEP' -1'UNTIL'1'DO'
          'BEGIN' A[R[K],C[J]] ← A[R[K],C[J]] - A[R[I],C[J]] ⁑ A[R[K],C[I]];
            'IF' K 'GR' I 'OR' J 'GR' I 'OR' ABS(A[R[K],C[J]]) 'GR' ABS(PIVOT)'THEN'
              'BEGIN' PIVI ← K; PIVJ ← J;
                PIVOT ← A[R[K],C[J]] 'END' CONDITIONAL
              'END' JLOOP;
                A[R[K],C[I]] ← -A[R[I],C[I]] ⁑ A[R[K],C[I]]
      'END' KLOOP
  'END'  ILOOP AND REDUCTION;
'COMMENT' REARRANGE ROWS;MATRIXPERM (A[J,P],A[K,P],J,K,R,C,N,P);
'COMMENT' REARRANGE COLUMNS;
  MATRIXPERM (A[P,J],A[P,K],J,K,C,R,N,P)
'END' MATRIXINVERT
```

NOTES:

This program has been included to illustrate the following:

1. general 'FOR' statements

2. a procedure statement which calls the procedure of Example 3.

Example: #5

Name: ARCCOSSIN

Origin: Communications of the ACM, September 1963, P 519, Algorithm 206

Author: Misako Konda, Japan Atomic Energy Research Institute, Tokai,
Tharaki, Japan

Problem

```
'PROCEDURE' ARCCOSSIN(X) RESULT:(ARCCOS,ARCSIN);
'VALUE' X;
'REAL' X, ARCCOS,ARCSIN;
'COMMENT' THIS PROCEDURE COMPUTES ARCCOS(X) AND ARCSIN(X) FOR
   -1'LQ'X'LQ'1.  THE CONSTANT 2 RAISED TO THE MINUS 27TH POWER
   DEPENDS ON THE WORD LENGTH AND RELATIVE MACHINE PRECISION,
   AND MAY BE REPLACED BY A VARIABLE IDENTIFIER.  ALARM IS THE
   PROCEDURE WHICH MESSAGES THAT X IS INVALID.
   THE APPROXIMATION FORMULA USED HERE WAS CODED FOR MUSA-
   SINO-1 IN ITS OWN LANGUAGE AT THE ELECTRICAL COMMUNICATION
   LABORATORY TOKYO.  THIS ALGORITHM WAS TRANSLATED INTO FAP AND
   SUCCESSFULLY RAN ON AN IBM 7090;
'BEGIN' 'REAL' A1, X1, X2, A2;  'INTEGER' R;
   'IF' ABS(X) 'GR' 1
   'THEN' 'GOTO' ALARM
   'ELSE' 'IF' ABS(X) 'GR' 2↑ (-27)
      'THEN' 'GOTO' L1
      'ELSE' 'BEGIN' ARCCOS ← 1.5707963; 'GOTO' L3
         'END';
L1:     'IF' X 'EQ' 1
        'THEN' 'BEGIN' ARCCOS ← 0; 'GOTO' L3
           'END'
        'ELSE' 'IF' X 'EQ' - 1
           'THEN' 'BEGIN' ARCCOS ← 3.1415926; 'GOTO' L3
              'END'
```

Example #5   (cont'd)

```
        'ELSE' 'BEGIN' A1 ← 0; X1 ← X;
            'FOR' R ← 0 'STEP' 1 'UNTIL' 26 'DO'
            'BEGIN' 'IF' X1 'LS' 0
                'THEN''BEGIN' A2 ← 1; X2 ← 1-2 ⁎ X1 ↑2 'END'
                'ELSE' 'BEGIN' A2 ← 0; X2 ← 2 ⁎ X1 ↑2 - 1 'END';
                A1 ← A1 + A2 ⁎ 2 ↑(-R-1);
                X1 ← X2
            'END';
        ARCCOS ← 3.1415926 ⁎ A1;
        'END':
L3:     ARCSIN ← 1.570963 - ARCCOS;
        'END' ARCCOSSIN
```

NOTES:

This program has been included to illustrate the following:

1.   procedure parameters separated by) letters: (

2.   a conditional statement containing several 'IF' clauses.

Example: #6

Name: SHELLSORT

Origin: Communications of the ACM, August 1963, P 445, Algorithm 201

Author: J. Boothroyd, English Electric-Leo Computers, Kidsgrove, Staffs, England

Problem

```
'PROCEDURE' SHELLSORT(A,N); 'VALUE' N; 'REAL''ARRAY' A; 'INTEGER' N;
'COMMENT' A[1] THROUGH A[N] OF A[1:N] ARE REARRANGED IN ASCENDING
    ORDER. THE METHOD IS THAT OF D.A.SHELL, (A HIGH-SPEED SORTING
    PROCEDURE, COMM. ACM 2 (1959), 30-32) WITH SUBSEQUENCES
    CHOSEN AS SUGGESTED BY T.N. HIBBERD (AN EMPIRICAL STUDY OF
    MINIMAL STORAGE SORTING, SDC REPORT SP-982). SUBSEQUENCES
    DEPEND ON M[1] THE FIRST OPERATIVE VALUE OF M. HERE M[1] EQUALS
    2↑ K-1  FOR 2↑K 'LQ' N 'LS' 2↑(K+1).  TO IMPLEMENT SHELL'S
    ORIGINAL CHOICE OF M[1] = [N/2] CHANGE THE FIRST STATEMENT
    TO M←N;
'BEGIN''INTEGER' I,J,K,M; 'REAL' W;
    'FOR' I ← 1 'STEP' I 'UNTIL' N 'DO' M ← 2 ⁎ I - 1;
    'FOR' M ← M % 2 'WHILE' M 'NQ' 0 'DO'
        'BEGIN' K ← N - M;
            'FOR' J ← 1 'STEP' 1 'UNTIL' K 'DO'
                'BEGIN' 'FOR' I ← J 'STEP' -M 'UNTIL' 1 'DO'
                    'BEGIN''IF' A[I+M] 'GQ' A[I] 'THEN' 'GOTO' L1;
                        W ← A[I]; A[I] ← A[I+M]; A[I+M] ← W;
                    'END' I;
            L1:'END' J
        'END' M
'END' SHELLSORT;
```

Example: #6 (cont'd)

NOTES:

This program has been included to illustrate the following:

1. a series of nested 'FOR' *statements*

2. a dummy statement (labelled L1).

226

Example: #7

Name: SMOOTH

Origin: Communications of the ACM, November 1963, P 663, Algorithm 216

Author: Richard George, Argonne National Laboratory, Argonne, Ill.

Problem

```
'PROCEDURE' SMOOTH (DATA) WHICH IS A LIST OF LENGTH: (N);
   'INTEGER' N; 'REAL''ARRAY' DATA;
   'BEGIN'
      'COMMENT' THIS PROCEDURE ACCOMPLISHES FOURTH-ORDER SMOOTH-
         ING OF A LIST USING THE METHOD GIVEN BY LANCZOS,"APPLIED
         ANALYSIS" (PRENTICE-HALL, 1956). THIS ALGORITHM REQUIRES ONLY
         ONE ADDITIONAL LIST FOR TEMPORARY STORAGE;
      'REAL' FACTOR, TOP; 'INTEGER' MAX I,I,J; 'ARRAY' DELTA [1:N];
      FACTOR ← 3.0/35.0;
      MAX I ← N - 1;
      'FOR' I ← 1 'STEP' 1 'UNTIL' MAX I 'DO'
         DELTA [I] ← DATA[I+1] - DATA [I];
      'FOR' J ← 1 'STEP' 1 'UNTIL' 3 'DO'
         'BEGIN'
            TOP ← DELTA[1];
            MAX I ← MAX I - 1;
            'FOR' I ← 1 'STEP' 1 'UNTIL' MAX I 'DO'
               DELTA [I] ← DELTA [I+1] - DELTA [I]
         'END';
      MAX I ← N - 2;
      'FOR' I ← 3 'STEP' 1 'UNTIL' MAX I 'DO'
         DATA [I] ← DATA [I] - DELTA [I-2] ⋇ FACTOR;
      DATA [1] ← DATA [1] + TOP/5.0 + DELTA [1] ⋇ FACTOR;
      DATA [2] ← DATA [2] - TOP ⋇ 0.4 - DELTA [1]/7.0;
```

Example: <u>#7</u> *(cont'd)*

```
    DATA [N] ← DATA [N] - DELTA [N-3]/5.0 + DELTA [N-4] * FACTOR;
    DATA [N-1] ← DATA [N-1] + DELTA [N-3] * 0.4 - DELTA [N-4]/7.0
'END';
```

<u>*NOTES:*</u>

This program has been included to illustrate the following:

1. *two procedure parameters separated by the sequence) letters: (instead of by a comma.*

Name: DETERMINANT

Origin: Communications of the ACM, March 1963, P 104, Algorithm 159

Author: David W. Digby, Oregon State University, Corvallis, Ore.

Problem

```
'REAL' 'PROCEDURE' DETERMINANT (X,N);
'VALUE' N; 'INTEGER' N; 'ARRAY' X;
'COMMENT' DETERMINANT CALCULATES THE DETERMINANT OF THE N-BY-
    N SQUARE MATRIX X, USING THE COMBINATORIAL DEFINITION OF THE
    DETERMINANT. THIS ALGORITHM IS INTENDED AS AN EXAMPLE OF A
    RECURSIVE PROCEDURE WHICH IS SOMEWHAT LESS TRIVIAL THAN FACTORIAL
    (ALGORITHM 33);
'BEGIN' 'REAL' D; 'INTEGER' I; 'BOOLEAN' 'ARRAY' B[1:N];
    'PROCEDURE' THREAD (P,E,I);
        'VALUE' P,E,I; 'REAL' P; 'INTEGER' E,I;
        'IF' I 'GR' N 'THEN' D ← D + P ⋇ (-1) ↑ E 'ELSE' 'IF' P 'NQ' 0 'THEN'
            'BEGIN' 'INTEGER' J,F;
                F ← 0;
                'FOR' J ← N 'STEP' -1 'UNTIL' 1 'DO'
                    'IF' B[J] 'THEN' F ← F + 1 'ELSE'
                        'BEGIN'
                            B[J] ← 'TRUE';
                            THREAD (P⋇X[I,J],E+F,I+1);
                            B[J] ← 'FALSE';
                        'END' OF LOOP;
            'END' OF THREAD;
    'FOR' I ← 1 'STEP' 1 'UNTIL' N 'DO'
        B[I] ← 'FALSE';
    D ← 0;
    THREAD (1,0,1);
    DETERMINANT ← D;
'END' DETERMINANT;
```

Example: #8 (cont'd)

<u>*NOTES:*</u>

This program has been included to illustrate the following:

1. a procedure, DETERMINANT, which is a function definition

2. a procedure, THREAD, which calls itself (recursive definition).

Example: #9

Name: NEWTON MAEHLY

Origin: *Communications of the ACM, July 1962, P 387, Algorithm 105*

Author: *F.L. Bauer and J. Stoer, Johannes Guttenberg-Universitat, Mainz, Germany*

Problem

```
'PROCEDURE' NEWTON MAEHLY (A,N,Z,EPS);
    'VALUE' N,EPS;
    'ARRAY' A,Z;
    'INTEGER' N;
    'REAL' EPS;
    'COMMENT' THE PROCEDURE DETERMINES ALL ZEROS Z[1:N] OF THE
        POLYNOMIAL P(X) ← A[0] ¨ X↑N + ... + A[N] OF ORDER N, IF P(X)
        HAS ONLY REAL ZEROS WHICH HAVE TO BE ALL DIFFERENT. THE ZEROS
        Z[I] ARE ORDERED ACCORDING TO THEIR MAGNITUDE: Z[1] 'GR' Z[2] 'GR'
        ... 'GR' Z[N]. THE APPROXIMATIONS FOR EACH ZERO WILL BE IMPROVED
        BY ITERATION AS LONG AS ABS(X1-X0) 'GR' EPS ¨ ABS(X1) HOLDS
        FOR TWO SUCCESSIVE APPROXIMATIONS X0 AND X1;
'BEGIN' 'REAL' AA,PP,QQ,X0,X1;
    'INTEGER' I,M,S;
    'ARRAY' B,P,Q[0:N-1];
    'PROCEDURE' HORNER(P,Q,N,X,PP,QQ);
        'VALUE' N,X;
        'ARRAY' P,Q;
        'REAL' PP,X,QQ;
        'INTEGER' N;
    'BEGIN''REAL' S,S1;
        'INTEGER' I;
        S ← S1 ← 0;
```

```
'FOR' I ← 0 'STEP' 1 'UNTIL' N-1 'DO'
'BEGIN' S ← S*X+P[I]; S1 ← S1*X+Q[I]; 'END';
PP ← S*X+P[N]; QQ ← S1;
'END';
P[0] ← AA ← A[0]; X0 ← PP ← 0; S ← SIGN(A[0]);
'FOR' I ← 1 'STEP' 1 'UNTIL' N 'DO'
    'IF' S * A[I]'LS'0 'THEN'
        'BEGIN' 'IF' PP'EQ'0 'THEN' PP ← I;
                'IF' X0'LS'ABS(A[I]) 'THEN' X0 ← ABS(A[I]);
        'END';
X0 ← 'IF' PP'EQ'0 'THEN' 0 'ELSE' 1+EXP(LN(ABS(X0/AA))/PP);
'COMMENT' X0 IS A FIRST APPROXIMATION FOR THE LARGEST ZERO WHICH
    MAY BE PRINTED OUT AT THIS POINT OF THE PROGRAM;
'FOR' I ← 0 'STEP' 1 'UNTIL' N-1 'DO' B[I] ← (N-1)*A[I];
'FOR' M ← 1 'STEP' 1 'UNTIL' N 'DO'
    'BEGIN'
    ITERATION:
    HORNER (A,B,N,X0,PP,QQ); X1 ← X0-PP/QQ;
    'IF' ABS(X1-X0)'GR'EPS*ABS(X1) 'THEN'
        'BEGIN' X0 ← X1;
            'COMMENT' X0 IS THE LAST APPROXIMATION FOR THE ZERO
                BEING IMPROVED, WHICH MAY BE PRINTED OUT AT THIS
                POINT;
            'GOTO' ITERATION;
        'END';
    Z[M] ← X1;
    'COMMENT' Z[M] ← X1 IS THE MTH ZERO OF THE POLYNOMIAL;
    PP ← B[0] ← B[0] - AA; Q[0] ← PP;
    'IF' M'LS'N 'THEN'
        'BEGIN' 'FOR' I ← 1 'STEP' 1 'UNTIL' N-1 'DO'
                'BEGIN' PP ← P[I] ← X1*P[I-1]+A[I];
```

Example: #9 *(cont'd)*

```
                        PP ← B[I] ← B(I)-PP;
                        Q[I] ← X1*Q[I-1]+PP;
                'END';
            HORNER (P,Q,N-1,X1,PP,QQ);
                X0 ← X1-PP/QQ;
            'COMMENT' X0 IS A FIRST APPROXIMATION FOR THE
                NEXT ZERO;
        'END'
    'END'
'END' NEWTON MAEHLY;
```

<u>*NOTES:*</u>

This program has been included to illustrate the following:

1. *a procedure declaration, HORNER, within another procedure declaration, NEWTON MAEHLY.*
2. *use of many mathematical functions.*

Example: #10

Name: GAUSS'S METHOD

Origin: Communications of the ACM, July 1962, P 388, Algorithm 107

Author: Jay W. Counts, University of Missouri, Columbia, Mo.

Problem

```
'PROCEDURE' GAUSS (U,A,Y);
'REAL' 'ARRAY' A,Y; 'REAL' TEMP; 'INTEGER' U;
'COMMENT' THIS PROCEDURE IS FOR SOLVING A SYSTEM OF
    LINEAR EQUATIONS BY SUCCESSIVE ELIMINATION OF THE UN-
    KNOWNS. THE AUGMENTED MATRIX IS A AND U THE NUMBER OF
    UNKNOWNS. THE SOLUTION VECTOR IS Y. IF THE SYSTEM HASN'T
    ANY SOLUTION OR MANY SOLUTIONS, THIS IS INDICATED BY
    'GOTO' STOP;
'BEGIN'
    'INTEGER' I,J,K,M,N;
    N ← 0;
CK0:  N ← N+1;
    'FOR' K ← N 'STEP' 1 'UNTIL' U 'DO' 'IF' A[K,N] 'NQ' 0 'THEN'
    'GOTO' CK1; 'GOTO' STOP;
CK1:  'IF' K'EQ'N 'THEN' 'GOTO' CK2;
    'FOR' M ← N 'STEP' 1 'UNTIL' U+1 'DO'
  'BEGIN'
    TEMP ← A[N,M]; A[N,M] ← A[K,M]; A[K,M] ← TEMP
  'END';
CK2:  'FOR' J ← U+1 'STEP'-1 'UNTIL' N 'DO' A[N,J] ← A[N,J]/A[N,N];
    'FOR' I ← K+1 'STEP' 1 'UNTIL' U 'DO'
    'FOR' J ← N+1 'STEP' 1 'UNTIL' U+1 'DO'
    A[I,J] ← A[I,J]-A[I,N]*A[N,J];
    'IF' N'NQ'U 'THEN' 'GOTO' CK0;
    'FOR' I ← U 'STEP'-1 'UNTIL' 1 'DO'
  'BEGIN'
```

Example: #10 (cont'd)

```
    Y[I] ← A[I,U+1]/A[I,I];
    'FOR' K ← I-1 'STEP'-1 'UNTIL' 1 'DO'
    A[K,U+1] ← A[K,U+1] A[K,I]``Y[I]
'END''END';
```

NOTES:

This program has been included to illustrate the following:

1. the statement "s" of a 'FOR' statement is another 'FOR' statement

Example: #11

Name: NEWTON INTERPOLATION WITH FORWARD DIVIDED DIFFERENCES

Origin: Communications of the ACM, April 1963, P 165, Algorithm 169

Author: W. Kahan and I. Farkas, Institute of Computer Science,
University of Toronto, Canada

Problem

```
'PROCEDURE' FNEWT(Z,N,X,F,R,D,E); 'VALUE' Z,N;
    'REAL' Z,R,D,E; 'INTEGER' N; 'REAL''ARRAY' X,F;
'COMMENT' X IS A REAL ARRAY OF DIMENSION AT LEAST N IN WHICH
    X[I] 'EQ' X[I] FOR I = 1,2,...,N. THE VALUES X[I] NEED NOT BE DIS-
    TINCT NOR IN ANY SPECIAL ORDER, BUT ONCE THE ARRAY X IS CHOSEN
    IT WILL FIX THE INTERPRETATION OF THE ARRAY F. F IS A REAL ARRAY
    OF DIMENSION AT LEAST N AND CONTAINS THE FORWARD DIVIDED
    DIFFERENCES F[I] = DELTA FUNCTION(X[1],X[2],...,X[I]) I = 1,2,...,N.
    IF TWO OR MORE OF THE VALUES X[I] ARE EQUAL THEN SOME OF THE F'S
    MUST BE CONFLUENT DIVIDED DIFFERENCES, SEE ALGORITHM: "CALCU-
    LATION OF CONFLUENT DIVIDED DIFFERENCES." (ACM, APRIL 1963, P 164).
    R IS THE VALUE OF THE FOLLOWING POLYNOMIAL IN Z OF DEGREE N-1 AT MOST
    F[1] + (Z-X[1])*(F[2] + (Z-X[2])*(F[3] + ... + (Z-X[N-1])*F[N])...)). THIS
    POLYNOMIAL IS AN INTERPOLATION POLYNOMIAL WHICH WOULD, BUT
    FOR ROUNDING ERRORS, MATCH VALUES OF THE FUNCTION F(X) AND ANY
    OF ITS DERIVATIVES THAT THE ABOVE ALGORITHM MIGHT HAVE BEEN GIVEN.
    D IS THE VALUE OF THE DERIVATIVE OF R. E IS THE MAXIMUM ERROR IN R
    CAUSED BY ROUNDOFF DURING THE EXECUTION OF FNEWT. THE ERROR
    ESTIMATE IS BASED UPON THE ASSUMPTION THAT THE RESULT OF EACH
    FLOATING-POINT ARITHMETIC OPERATION IS TRUNCATED TO 27 SIGNIFICANT
    BINARY DIGITS AS IS THE CASE IN FORTRAN PROGRAMS ON THE 7090.
    FNEWT HAS BEEN WRITTEN AS A FORTRAN II SUBROUTINE AND IS
    AVAILABLE FROM I.C.S., UNIVERSITY OF TORONTO;
```

Example: #11 *(cont'd)*

```
'BEGIN''REAL' Z1; 'INTEGER' I;
R ← D ← E ← 0;
'FOR' I ← N 'STEP'  1 'UNTIL' 1 'DO'
'BEGIN'
Z1 ← Z - X[I];
D ← R + Z1 * D;
R ← F[I] + Z1*R;
E ← ABS(R) + ABS(Z1)*E
'END';
E ← (1.5*E - ABS(R))*3'-8
'END' FNEWT
```

Notes:

This program has been included to illustrate the following:

1. a real number written with an exponent

Appendix 4
Glossary of Terms

(Note:

In certain cases, a term which has not yet been defined may be used in a definition. This occurs because of the decision to present the glossary in alphabetic order for reference purposes.)

1. *arithmetic*
   expression:

   Either a simple arithmetic expression or an 'IF'
   clause arithmetic expression.

2. *Boolean*
   expression:

   Either a simple Boolean expression or an 'IF'
   clause Boolean expression.

3. *conditional*
   designator:

   A clause of the form 'IF' *b* 'THEN' *c* 'ELSE' *d,*
   where b represents a Boolean expression, c
   may be either a statement label, a switch
   designator, or a conditional designator enclosed
   within parentheses, and d may be either a state-
   ment label, a switch designator, or a conditional
   designator (which need not be enclosed within
   parentheses).

4. *designational*
   expression:

   A statement label, a switch designator, or a
   conditional designator.

5. *expression:*

   Either an arithmetic expression or a Boolean
   expression.

6. *identifier:*

   A name given to a variable, an array, a label,
   a switch, a procedure. The name may be composed
   of any number of letters and digits. However,
   the name must begin with a letter.

   Example:
   A, BETA, M12, T12C7, TOTALAMOUNT

6. *identifier:*
    (cont'd)

Blanks are not considered significant in ALGOL except in strings, and they may be used freely within identifiers.

Example:
    AB LE *is considered the same identifier as* ABLE *or* ABL E.

Two different quantities may not have the same identifier unless they appear in different blocks. (See the section COMPOUND STATEMENTS AND BLOCKS for clarification.) Certain identifiers are reserved for standard procedures by the ALGOL compiler. (See the list of reserved identifiers in Appendix I.)

7. 'IF' *clause arithmetic expression:*

'IF' *a* 'THEN' *b* 'ELSE' *c, where a is a Boolean expression, b is a simple arithmetic expression, and c is either a simple arithmetic expression or an* 'IF' *clause arithmetic expression.*

The 'IF' *clause arithmetic expression causes one of several arithmetic expressions to be evaluated on the basis of the value of Boolean expressions.*

The expression to be evaluated is selected as follows:
a) *The Boolean expressions are evaluated one by one in sequence from left to right until one having a value* 'TRUE' *is found.*

7.	'IF' *clause* *arithmetic* *expression:* *(cont'd)*	b) *The value of the* 'IF' *clause arithmetic expression is the value of the first simple arithmetic expression following this Boolean expression.*
8.	'IF' *clause* *Boolean* *expression:*	'IF' *a* 'THEN' *b* 'ELSE' *c, where b is a simple Boolean expression and a and c are either simple Boolean expressions or* 'IF' *clause Boolean expressions.*
		The 'IF' *clause Boolean expression is evaluated in the same way as an* 'IF' *clause arithmetic expression.*
9.	*integer:*	*A whole number written without a decimal point.*
		Positive integers may have no sign or may be preceded by a plus sign. Negative integers must be preceded by a minus sign.
		Example: 0, −452, +7586421, 33
10.	*number:*	*Integer, real number.*
11.	*real number:*	*A series of decimal digits written with or without a decimal point. If the decimal point appears it must not be the last character.*

11. *real number:*
    (cont'd)

An exponent part may be added to specify the integral power of 10 to which the number must be raised. The exponent part is separated from the digits by an apostrophe ('). The exponent may also appear alone.

Positive real numbers do not require a sign. However, a plus sign is permitted. Negative real numbers require a minus sign.

Example:
    15.7, -.0045, +25.0, 1.7'-3, 5'3

12. *simple*
    arithmetic
    expression:

A sequence of numbers, variables, subscripted variables or function calls separated by arithmetic operators and parentheses, which represents a rule for computing a numerical value.

Rules:
1. All quantities used in an arithmetic expression must be of type real or integer.

2. For operators +, - or *, the result of calculation will be integer if both operands are integer, otherwise real.

3. There are 2 operators which denote division / and %.

    a) / is defined for all combinations of real and integer, and will always give a result of type real.

12. *simple*
    arithmetic
    expression:
    (cont'd)

b) *% is defined only for operands of type integer and will always give a result of type integer. The result is truncated, not rounded to an integer, i.e., 5 % 3 = 1.*

4. *Exponentiation*

   a) *a↑b↑c is equivalent to $(a^b)^c$.*

   b) *The types of the base and the exponent may be any combination of real and integer.*

   c) *If the exponent is an integer, the result is as follows:*

exp	base	result
>0	all	same type as base
=0	≠0	same type as base
=0	=0	operation is undefined
<0	≠0	real
<0	=0	operation is undefined

12. *simple arithmetic expression: (cont'd)*

d) *If the exponent is a real number, the result is as follows:*

exp	base	result
>0		
=0	>0	real
<0		
>0	=0	real
≤0	=0	operation is undefined
>0		
=0	<0	operation is undefined
<0		

5. *Hierarchy of operators -*
   1. *exponentiation* ↑

   2. *multiplication & division * / %*

   3. *addition & subtraction + -*

6. *Expressions inside parentheses are evaluated first.*

7. *Evaluation proceeds basically from left to right within the hierarchy and within parentheses. Function calls and parenthesized quantities are evaluated from left to right.*

13. *simple*
    Boolean
    expression:
A sequence of variables, subscripted variables, function calls and relations possibly separated by logical operators and parentheses, which represents a rule for computing a logical value (i.e., 'TRUE' or 'FALSE').

Rules:

1. Variables and functions used with the logical operators must be declared to be of type Boolean.

2. A relation is composed of two arithmetic expressions separated by a relational operator.

    Example:
        A-B*C 'EQ' Z*Y

3. A relation has a value of 'TRUE' if the relation is satisfied otherwise it has a value of 'FALSE'.

4. The logical operators are defined as follows:

    a) 'NOT' a is true or false if a is false or true, respectively.

    b) a 'AND' b is true if both a and b are true, otherwise it is false.

    c) a 'OR' b is false if both a and b are false, otherwise it is true.

13. *simple Boolean expression:*
    (cont'd)

d) *a* 'IMP' *b is false if a is true and b is false, otherwise it is true.*

e) *a* 'EQV' *b is true if either both a and b are true or both are false, otherwise it is false.*

5. *The hierarchy of operations in evaluating a Boolean expression is as follows:*

    1. *arithmetic operators - same as for arithmetic expressions*

    2. *relational operators - all on same level*

    3. *logical operators*

6. *The hierarchy of logical operators is:*

    1. 'NOT'

    2. 'AND'

    3. 'OR'

    4. 'IMP'

    5. 'EQV'

7. *Expressions inside parentheses are evaluated first.*

14. *simple statement:*   A statement which is not a compound statement
                            or a block.

                            Examples:

                                assignment

                                conditional

                                dummy

                                'FOR'

                                'GO TO'

                                procedure

15. *statement*   An identifier placed before a statement.
     label:

                            A statement label must be followed by a colon
                            to separate the label from the statement.

                            A statement may have more than one label, each
                            one followed by a colon.

| 15. | statement label: (cont'd) | Statement labels are used so that a statement may be referenced. |

15. statement
     label:
       (cont'd)

Statement labels are used so that a statement may be referenced.

Examples:

1) AB: A←B

2) AC: 'BEGIN' A←C 'END'

3) AD: 'BEGIN' AE: A←E 'END'

4) AF: AG: AH: A←H;

16. string:

A sequence of basic symbols enclosed in the left and right string quotes (" and \); or a sequence of basic symbols and strings enclosed in the string quotes.

Strings may be used as actual parameters of procedures.

Examples of strings:
  "A B C\
  " A B " CDE\FG\

17. subscripted
     variable:

A subscripted variable has the form $a[b_1, b_2, \ldots, b_n]$ where a is an array identifier and $b_1, b_2, \ldots, b_n$ are subscripts.

A subscript may be any arithmetic expression, and the number of subscripts, n, must be the same as the number of dimensions declared for a.

17.	*subscripted variable:* *(cont'd)*	*Each subscript* b_i *acts like a variable of type* 'INTEGER' *and the evaluation of the subscript is equivalent to using the function* ENTIER $(h_i + .5)$.

Evaluation of subscripts within a subscript list proceeds from left to right. The value of the subscripted variable is defined only if the value of each subscript expression is within the subscript bounds of the array.

Example:

```
AB[1,3], BOY['IF' B 'EQ' C 'THEN' 1 'ELSE' 2]
```

18.	*switch designator:*	$sw[a]$, *where sw represents a switch identifier and a represents an arithmetic expression.*

19.	*variable:*	*A quantity referred to by a name (the variable identifier) whose value may be changed.*

The kind of quantity a variable may represent is determined by a type declaration and may be either integer, real or Boolean.

Example:

```
X, ABC, YZ5N,
THIS IS A VARIABLE
```